Endorsements!

"What I wouldn't give to have had this book while I was building the UGG brand! As I was reading *The Belief Zone*, I remembered my own creation process with UGG and wished I'd had these insights along the way. When I first started selling the boots, I was terrified, and I really had to confront my limiting beliefs about selling and about myself! If you feel stuck in your business growth right now, and you feel like you've read every self-development book out there, then this book is for you. Ursula will help you confront your limiting beliefs and she will show you how you can step into a New Belief Zone that will allow you to create the goals you've been thinking about for a long time.

On a personal note, I'm also really glad I met Ursula before building my speaking brand. She helped me bust through some of my limiting beliefs in just one short conversation and a few weeks later, I was standing on her stage, delivering my first keynote! And since then, I'm paid more than I thought possible at that time for a keynote, and I'm able to witness the impact

I have on the audience. Let Ursula help you bust through your limiting beliefs today!"

Brian Smith

Founder of UGG Boots and Author of Birth of a Brand

"Get ready to have the most major life shifts ever when you read the Belief Zone! This is truly a transformational experience where you will finally realize your desires. I love the process and you will, too, as you create your own Belief Zone Blueprint - totally brilliant! Are you ready to live the life you have been dreaming of? It's your time now - grab a copy of the Belief Zone."

Terri Levine

Chief Heartrepreneur™, and best-selling author of Turbocharge: How To Transform Your Business As A Heartrepreneur™.

"Keep this book within reach at all times and refer to it often. It will make the difference between settling for an average life or creating the life of your dreams and doing your life's work."

Mark LeBlanc

Author of Never Be the Same and Growing Your Business!

"Ursula Mentjes hits the reader spot on and magical break-throughs happen! She truly dives into mindset and beliefs and helps people transform into being more confident, successful and fulfilled. I highly recommend this book for life changing results!"

Kim Somers Egelsee

 # 1 Bestselling Author of Living The Ten+ Life

"If you want your business to explode, then read the cutting-edge new book, *The Belief Zone,* by best-selling author, Business Woman of the Year and recipient of the Lifetime Achievement Award from the President of the United States of America, Ursula Mentjes!"

Lynn Perterson Jungblut

CEO of Speakers Engagements and Events

"*The Belief Zone* is amazing! Ursula Mentjes has found a way to bring Quantum Physics and sales together in an easy to understand, yet profound manner. I was able to plug in my own information to the material to shift my beliefs, too. Thank you, Ursula!"

Leisa Reid, Productive Learning

"I have been observing Ursula's work for years and she is truly one of the great minds in the field of sales and marketing. I am recommending to all business owners that they strongly consider reading her new book *The Belief Zone,* and learn from one of the great sales and marketing genius of our times."

Dennis S. Watts, Research Scientist, Quantum Physics

"Ursula Mentjes has done it again! With her "The Belief Zone" along with her previous books *"Selling with Intention", "Selling with Synchronicity"* and *"One Great Goal",* she has captured the essence of what it takes to be successful.

Today's Sales Professional and Entrepreneur will gain a new understanding of what it takes to believe in oneself and their product or service. Ursula has a great way of communicating to the reader the fundamentals for building your business to the greatest heights that you can ever imagine.

I love systems, and Ursula has crafted a Seven Step System that is making a difference in the way I look at and believe when it comes to my business. Step #4, "Shift", has me thinking and will get the reader thinking in a new/dynamic way that will blow the competition away!

In these highly competitive times, we must shift the way we think/do/act in our business and Ursula presents it in an easy to understand method that anyone can incorporate into their way of doing business. If there was ever a recommendation to get a book, it would be for *"The Belief Zone"*. Get your copy today!

Maurice DiMino, Two-Time #1 Bestselling Author,
Creator of the W.I.N. at Leadership Method and Elevate
Your Authority System.

"If you believe in you, if you believe you are worthy, but just haven't reached your potential, then you should believe in *The Belief Zone.* Packed with a combination of inspiration and information, it shows YOU how to get in the right frame of mind to achieve your dreams."

Liz Goodgold, Founder of RedFire Branding
and the Author of RedFire Branding

"So powerful! *The Belief Zone* will challenge you to embrace the amount of control you have pertaining to what happens in your life. I recognizing and removing barriers, you will have the tools to create a road map to what's possible. *The Belief Zone* has helped me realize that I hold my breath when I think of the good things that are possible in my life. Learning to "shift" is now as easy as remembering how to breathe."

Janise Graham, Speaker, Author, Insurance Strategist and founder of Entrepreneurs Insurance Services

"So powerful! *The Belief Zone* will challenge you to embrace the amount of control you have pertaining to what happens in your life. I recognizing and removing barriers, you will have the tools to create a road map to what's possible. *The Belief Zone* has helped me realize that I hold my breath when I think of the good things that are possible in my life. Learning to "shift" is now as easy as remembering how to breathe."

Janise Graham, Speaker, Author, Insurance Strategist and founder of Entr

"Once in a while you find a book that has it all—a real success story and a easy to follow formula to duplicate the author's success. That's *The Belief Zone*. How do I know? Because there are success stories inside of people who have done just that. Even better? It is customized FOR YOU because Ursula shows you exactly how to change your beliefs about money, sales, success and more.

If you feel stuck, ready to give up or just tired of "things always being the same", then you need to read *The Belief Zone*. This is your opportunity to make a profound and lasting change in your professional and personal life."

Justin Sachs, International Best-Selling Author of 8 books including The Power of Persistence

"Breakthrough after breakthrough awaits when you give yourself permission to enter *The Belief Zone*. More than a book, Ursula Mentjes helps you create a way of being that changes all aspects of your life, including your business and the way you make money. In the first few pages I realized I had not been living my joy for several years in spite of success and teaching others to see and live theirs. That awareness has changed the way I look at daily choices. I now catch myself when thoughts of "this energy, abundance, etc. won't last and focus on the now and can see my soul purpose coming to me again. Don't wait another minute, get The Belief Zone and shift your thinking today!"

Laura Steward, Founder Wisdom Learned, LLC, iHeart Radio Host, #1 International and Nautilus Award winning Author of What Would a Wise Woman Do?

"This wonderful book gives you the magic key that explains and creates success (or failure) in every area of your life. The power of belief is so strong and under your control, once you have it, your future becomes unlimited."

Brian Tracy – Speaker, Author, Trainer – 82 books

"If you've been wishing for something greater or better in your life (more money, better clients more time off), or if you've been struggling to achieve your goals, Ursula Mentjes' new book, *The Belief Zone,* can help. Ursula always inspires, and this book shows how to effortlessly discover your goals (the ones you truly desire), move out of your comfort zone, and step into a new 'Belief Zone' where your desires are waiting for you. As Ursula says, 'Don't wait...begin to BELIEVE again!' and this book will show you how."

Jean-Noel Bassior, Speaker Services

THE BELIEF ZONE

A Blueprint to Make More Money,
Give Back to the Organizations You Care About,
and Live an Authentic Life

Includes the Popular One Great Goal Process!

URSULA C. MENTJES

LEADERS IN GLOBAL PUBLISHING

Published by Motivational Press, Inc.
1777 Aurora Road
Melbourne, Florida, 32935
www.MotivationalPress.com

Manufactured in the United States of America.

ISBN: 978-1-62865-439-4

CONTENTS

ACKNOWLEDGMENTS

THE BELIEF ZONE, like my other books, was a labor of love shared by many! And I could not have written it without the amazing support of so many, including my amazingly cool husband Tim, my Mom, my Editor and Book Coach Amanda Johnson, Rebekah Hall, Lynn Wakefield, and my family and dear friends— you know who you are. A special thank you to our son, Lucca, for reminding me that life is precious and every moment counts.

Thank you to Justin Sachs and the entire team at Motivational Press. I am so grateful for your belief in this book and in me! And, Terri Levine, for so being so willing to make the introduction to Justin and so generous with your knowledge and connections.

To my Creator: Thank you for sending me to the planet at this time and for giving us all such powerful and creative abilities.

Thank you to my team at Sales Coach Now, The True to Intention Team, and the Tenacious Team.

Thank you to everyone at the National Association of Women Business Owners, Business Resource Connection, Polka Dot Powerhouse, and eWomen Network for all of their ongoing support.

And last, but never least, to my dear Sales Camp and Synchronize Clients—I wrote this for you. Your emails, social media messages, and love keep me inspired to help even more people break through those Limiting Beliefs so they can MAKE A LOT OF MONEY, give back to the organizations they care about, AND live a great life. You are ALL bright lights on a planet that desperately needs you to shine right NOW.

For Lucca.
You made us believe.

FOREWORD

By Greg Kuhn

A FEW YEARS AGO, Ursula challenged me to explore how the belief raising process I teach in my books can help salespeople. I was thrilled to speak with this extremely smart, compassionate, driven sales coach who was not only applying the principles of quantum physics to the business and entrepreneur sector, but also sharing them with others from stages and through books.

When she asked me to write this foreword, I was flattered. How could I not be? And I was also excited. Our last conversation had sparked the idea for a book, *Why Quantum Physicists Play "Grow a Greater You"* – where might this conversation take me? Well, it sparked another book!

Ursula didn't tell me what my next book should be about, but our conversations helped me begin to see it.

And that kind of inspiration awaits you here.

After personal access to Ursula, this is the next best thing. *The Belief Zone* is an extended literary conversation full of great ideas.

When a professional like Ursula puts everything she has into something, it's going to be valuable. When a teacher like Ursula roots her lessons in science, they can help transform you. I can't guarantee your results, but I'd be willing to wager that the ideas she shares in this book will inspire some great experiences and powerful shifts for you... *if you apply them.*

Like Ursula, I teach people how to exert greater influence over their beliefs, and appearing on Ursula's podcast and writing this foreword helped me to see some new wrinkles to hacking our software and building beliefs that can help us sell more and make almost any experience better. I thought I'd share them here, as it's likely that you'll face one or both of them as you journey through this book and begin to apply the principles so powerfully laid out for you. Wrinkle number one is defensiveness, a red-light indicator that you might be unaware of some fear or anger lurking beneath the surface. Wrinkle number two is not allowing yourself to feel as scared or angry as you'll allow yourself, as it usually gives you more control over your state of being. As you'll see on these pages, the more you can control your state of being, the more you can influence any experience.

Those insights might just give birth to an entire book. And Ursula helped me get to them by asking really great questions. Half the time, asking better questions is the key to breakthroughs and Ursula knows how to get right to the heart of things.

I won't be surprised if Ursula helps you better understand concepts and ideas that you may never have connected to growing your business and doubling or tripling your sales. But insights aren't all you'll glean here. In *The Belief Zone,* Ursula provides you with strategies, techniques, and tools that will help you apply the principles of creation while you read. If you're open to growing yourself into a more successful salesperson, you've made a wise decision to invest yourself here.

You are holding a book built upon science, written by a professional who cares, filled with ideas and strategies that inspire.

Time to dive in and grow!

Greg Kuhn

Author of the best-selling Why Quantum Physicists...Series

A NOTE FROM THE AUTHOR

WHAT IF YOU REALLY could double your sales or income in 90 days? What would be different in your business? In your life?

What would you need to believe to give yourself permission to launch a personal journey that takes you into a completely New Belief Zone?

When I was writing my last book, *Selling With Synchronicity*, my Book Coach and Editor, Amanda Johnson, said, "Do you know you talk about The Belief Zone over and over again in this book?" I realized I had started using the term The Belief Zone whenever I mentioned a Comfort Zone, and it really resonated with my clients and me. What I didn't realize was the impact of those three words on my own journey and the journey of others.

I'd like to invite YOU on a journey to explore how possible it is to double your sales in 90 days and create the life you've been dreaming of. On this journey, we will explore the power of your beliefs and expectations and how they impact every aspect of your sales—and life—success. I will also share with you The Belief Zone Blueprint, which is designed to keep you in The Belief Zone until you reach your stretch goals.

You are more powerful than you have ever imagined. You have the power to create a magical life and the utmost sales success that you could ever imagine! As you read this book, I want you to dream bigger than you have ever dreamed before. I want you to expect more than you have ever expected. And most of all, I want you to believe in a way that you have never believed before.

Welcome to The Belief Zone.

To Your Sales Success,

Ursula

Ursula Mentjes, M.S.

"The Sales Coach"

Sales Coach Now

Contact@SalesCoachNow.com

www.SalesCoachNow.com

www.MySalesCoachNow.com

INTRODUCTION

*"Twenty years from now, you will be more disappointed by the things
that you didn't do than by the ones you did do.
So throw off the bowlines. Sail away from the safe harbor.
Catch the trade winds in your sails. Explore. Dream. Discover."*

~ Mark Twain ~

I REMEMBER THE MOMENT I first believed I could make $50,000 per year. I was twenty-three years old. I had just landed a job as an outside sales professional, and with a $24,000 base salary plus commission, my manager told me I could probably make $50,000 per year. For me, at that age, that amount of money was like winning the lottery. Looking back, I can see how that thought—that belief—morphed into an expectation and then transformed firmly into reality.

I also remember the first time I believed I could make $100,000 in one year. I was the Branch Manager of the Santa Ana location of a Computer Training and Consulting Company. My salary (after a few other raises) had been bumped to $65,000 per year plus commission on anything I sold, and I would also earn a percentage on the overall sales of my team. Bingo! On my way to $100,000.

And then there was the $1,000,000 mark. I remember the first time I grew a branch from almost nothing to $83,333 per month, which led to my first $1,000,000 revenue year. And eventually, I learned how to have "$1,000,000 months" and more. At the same time, our personal net worth climbed over a $1,000,000.

The real question is, what did I have to believe to make that happen? And what did I have to believe when it all came crashing down? And then, what did I have to believe to bring it all back?

When I look back, I see that there were key moments that occurred in the beginning of this wild journey—like my manager telling me how much I could "expect" to make—that allowed me to take on new beliefs and effectively step into a New Belief Zone.

Back then, I didn't understand the power of belief, expectation, and knowing—I hadn't yet studied it. But I was doing it without knowing how. I had already stepped into a New Belief Zone that allowed me to reach the goals that I had. When I look back, I can see how my peers and supervisors largely influenced my New Belief Zone. Jim Rohn said we become the average of the five people we hang around the most. And that was the positive impact for me. Even though I didn't know HOW I was going to reach those goals, the power of the beliefs of the people around me was largely influential because they acted like it was simply the next step. "Everyone makes six figures in this industry." The power of their knowing helped launch me into a New Belief Zone.

The question for you is: What do YOU have to believe to reach your sales and income goals and your dream life? And, who is influencing your beliefs the most?

Whatever you believe about sales people, or whatever the Limiting Belief is you have about sales people or money, is the exact belief that will stop you from getting the sales you desire. And not having money will stop you from living the life of your dreams. Believe me, I've been on both sides!

Have you ever wished you could create the life of your dreams but you just haven't known where to begin? You keep thinking, *"If I could just sell more, if I just had more money, everything would be fine."* I remember feeling like that many times as I stumbled through my early life and career.

And there have been many times since then when I have ruminated on even bigger questions, wondering about my purpose and dreams—*"Am I on the right track? Am I living my purpose?"* And sometimes, *"Why are we even here on planet earth? What is this journey about when there is so much poverty, pain, and loss for so many people?"* Yes, there are times when my questions drive me a bit crazy. Can you relate? Monte Farber, in *Quantum Affirmations*, tells us that if you know your questions, then you know your answers. You just really need to ask some good questions.

My second book, *One Great Goal*, helped me answer some of those questions for myself as well as for my clients. We looked deeply into our Soul Purpose—why we are here, who we are serving, and how we are making a difference. I was reminded that our Soul Purpose isn't way outside of what we are doing now. In fact, it's part of everything we've done since we showed up on this planet. Our Soul Purposes are the culmination of every desire and experience to this point and will continue after this point. The key is to be listening to the "whispers" because we are always being guided by a "knowing" more powerful than us; we just aren't always listening. When the whispers turn to screams, we can't help but listen. For me, it was my health. I knew it was time to leave Corporate America when the chronic shingles on my neck simply would not go away. So I left and haven't looked back since.

What's your Soul whispering to you about your journey?

After I left Corporate America, my first big dream was to start my own business. I didn't think I could do it, but I also didn't feel like I had a choice because after growing a business to $20 million in annual revenue at twenty-seven years old, I had become highly unemployable. I either wanted to be the President of the next $20 million company or I needed to start my own company. Recruiters tired of me very quickly.

Once I was out on my own, in my own business, my entire belief system was challenged. For those of you who have started your own business or are commissioned sales professionals, you know what I am talking about! One day you have a steady paycheck and the next day you don't. It happens that fast. And when you realize that the income of your company (or your career) begins and ends with you, it can be a rude awakening. It certainly was for me!

What I didn't understand in the beginning was the power of clarity. I thought I knew what I wanted. I'd picture it in my mind. I'd daydream about it. But I only wrote a few goals down and I definitely didn't tell anyone. I didn't want anyone to judge me for my big goals. After all, what if I told someone and they didn't believe me, or told me I couldn't do it? So, I kept my dreams quiet. And my dreams didn't just include sales or business goals, of course. They also included dreams about my personal life. Deep down, I knew that my mission was to help entrepreneurs and sales professionals make a lot of money so they could give back to the organizations they care about AND live a great life. Pretty simple. But how the heck could I make that happen when I was struggling to pay my bills?

As I was working on becoming an NLP Certified Coach, getting my Master's Degree in Psychology, and launching my business, I learned quite a bit about goal achievement and creation. While doing all three things at the same time was challenging, it made me realize the importance of writing things down and telling someone we trust about our goals—getting committed—and how that can make a big difference in actually achieving our dreams.

While writing down my goals and telling select others (others who could support me) about them increased my motivation to achieve, I found that there were some goals that were more difficult. And I wasn't sure why. For example, my financial goals weren't happening as quickly as I wanted them to and I couldn't point to a reason. After all, I had easily created million-dollar lines of revenue for someone else—why couldn't I do it for myself?

I discovered the answer to that question in my training at the NLP Institute of California. What I learned was that my beliefs about myself (whether I deserved to earn that much money myself), and the belief that I had to work hard to make a lot of money, were holding me back. There were other beliefs within those that were keeping me stuck as well. In other words, I was running on old programs and Limiting Beliefs that stopped me from achieving the success that I desired in my own business.

So what did I do? I read every book I could find on Limiting Beliefs and dug deep into my NLP training to figure out the fastest and easiest way to change them so then I could also help my clients do the same. It started to work! As I changed my beliefs about myself, money, and other areas of my life, my business began to grow and I didn't have to work so hard anymore.

As I continued down this path, my husband's beliefs started to shift as a by-product of me talking about it all of the time, and we began to take more and more risks in real estate. There were times when I questioned how much risk we were taking on, but I just kept thinking that by staying on top of our investments and staying committed to our goals, everything would work out fine.

But it didn't.

When the Great Recession hit, we were impacted like many other people in California and other parts of the United States. In hindsight, maybe we should have admitted to ourselves that the crash was coming, but our egos desire status quo and safety, so it's easier to ignore the signs that are all around us than change course and trust the flow. Because we were holding so much real estate, we were impacted really hard. As the real estate values came crashing down, so did our portfolio. Bankruptcy was staring us in the face. But maybe, just maybe, we shouldn't have bought in to the depths of the doom and gloom. I'll admit that I bought it all—hook, line, and sinker. In the deepest part of the recession, I would hear other people saying that they weren't participating in the recession. I wanted that to be me as well, until I would look at all of the mortgages we couldn't pay. Somehow I had allowed my deepest fear to become my reality.

For five years, we dug ourselves out of a gigantic mess of real estate and other debt. Although we never filed bankruptcy, we certainly could have. And I'm not judging anyone who has or did file bankruptcy during the Great Recession. For us, we knew we had something serious to learn and, frankly, we were making enough money that we could, and should, pay those debts down. We decided that the right thing for us to do was to pay back as much of the debt as we could and negotiate other aspects of it.

We didn't come out without major cuts and bruises to our egos, our psyches and, of course, our financial situation. We learned valuable lessons along the way—wisdom that I want to share with you in this book. The truth is that as we dug out of the "mess," we learned more than we ever wanted to know about ourselves (the dark side), what was most important (God, faith, family, friends, and purpose), and why staying on our path and living into our Soul Purpose is so critical to this journey on earth, and critical to creating the life we desire.

Over time we did dig out, and creating a better life got easier and easier; and now we live in an incredible flow of synchronicity which allows us to create whatever we desire *as long as it's in alignment with our beliefs, values, and highest good.*

Does "being in the flow" mean that everything in my life is "perfect"? Well, that depends on what you believe about perfection, doesn't it? I've learned to reframe (an NLP term) what perfection really means in my life. Now, perfection is living a harmonious and interesting life where I am able to embrace the highs and the lows that come my way. I have surrounded myself with friends and professionals (Coaches, NLP Practitioners, Healers, etc.) who support me on my journey when I get stuck. I've learned to manage my thoughts and frequency so I am clear on what I am creating, wanted and unwanted, before I create it. And that's what I love to help my clients do—release their Limiting Beliefs, reprogram their minds for success, and achieve their greatest sales goals and whatever their *aligned* desires might be.

By the way, I might throw around some words like "frequency" and you might think to yourself, "Wow, she's pretty woo-woo." However, the application of Quantum Physics (knowingly or unknowingly) is becoming more and more mainstream as we continue to ask questions about how things really do come into creation in our lives and the impact our thoughts, behaviors, and expectations have on outcomes. In this book, we will explore the science behind the words that in the past have been described as "meta-physical" because I want to show you what Science is telling us. According to The American Heritage® New Dictionary of Cultural Literacy, Third Edition, *frequency* is defined as *"In physics, the number of crests of a wave that move past a given point in a given unit of time. The most common unit of frequency is the hertz (Hz), corresponding to one crest per second. The frequency of a wave can be calculated by dividing the speed of the wave by the wavelength. Thus, in the electromagnetic spectrum, the wavelengths decrease as the frequencies increase, and vice versa."*

Nikola Tesla, an American Serbian physicist (July 1856-January 1943), said, "If you want to find the secrets of the Universe, think in terms of energy, frequency and vibration."

Your thoughts and emotions have their own frequency because they are vibrational waves. Pam Grout said it perfectly in *E-Squared*, "That's what your thoughts are—vibrational energy waves that interact and influence the FP (field of potentiality). Every thought you have, have ever had, or ever will have creates a vibration that goes out into the FP, extending forever. These vibrations meet other vibrations, crisscrossing in an incredible maze of energy. Get enough energy together and it clumps into matter. Remember what Einstein said—matter is formed out of energy."

Over the past couple of years, I have been fortunate to create even faster than I have in the past. I will show you some of the things I've been able to create, and "how" I did it (which could be different for everyone), and also what I had to believe to make it happen. The "how" then became part of the exciting new technology I am going to share with you in The Belief Zone Blueprint. Don't worry—it's much easier than you might imagine! Often the most difficult part is just getting started, but we can help you with that, too. My intention is to help you see how my creation process works so you might be able to apply it to your own sales, business, and life.

MANIFESTATION VS. CREATION

Before we do that, though, I'd like to define a few more terms for you. The word *manifestation* is used a lot, but for some reason it never really resonated with me. I heard people saying it, and I thought I understood what it meant; but upon exploration, I really didn't. Merriam Webster defines *manifest* as, "*readily perceived by the senses and especially by the sense of sight; easily understood or recognized by the mind.*"

I always thought that manifest meant to "create" something— from start to finish. But after reading the definition, it didn't feel complete to me. "Perceived by the senses" didn't seem like enough. I didn't just want to "perceive" something with my senses, I wanted it to clearly be in my reality—front and center!

When I bring goals into reality, I create them—and so do you. We are all powerful creators. Merriam Webster defines creation as, *"to bring into existence—God* created *the heaven and the earth — Genesis 1:1(Authorized Version)."* Yes! That is what goal setting and realization really mean to me—creation! God just didn't visualize the heavens and the earth—He created them. God created us to be creative as well. (Note: Whatever you believe about God or Spirituality is up to you. Please insert those words that are meaningful to you.) Think about all of the things you have created (good and bad) in your life. When you were a child, you created things all of the time without even thinking about it. When you reframe the word "manifest" to "create," it instantly reminds you that YOU can create whatever you want. No goal is too big! Can you feel the difference?

Now, I am going to share what I created in just the past couple of years.

Caution: As you read my list, I do NOT want you to compare it to your own life and pass judgment on yourself or think you have to create anything that is on my list. This list is in alignment with my values and my beliefs. Remember, I've been working on this "creation stuff" for a long time and I'm going to teach you how to do it as well in The Belief Zone, particularly in the area of sales, but you can apply it to any area in your life!

So as you read this list, I want you to let it inspire you to begin to dream again.

Pay special attention to the beliefs that I needed to have inside of the creation process. Later in the book, as I define The Belief Zone, I will share how you can release Limiting Beliefs and then connect new beliefs to your focused expectations for ultimate results.

WHAT I CREATED IN THE PAST COUPLE OF YEARS

Created ALL NEW programs in my business. At the end of 2012, I could feel a shift happening with my clients and in my business. I knew that I needed to create the next level of programs to help my clients take the quantum leaps they desired. But my Limiting Belief was that changing again would hurt my brand. So, with the help of some of my new team members, we redesigned my entire program and re-launched in 2013. This is when our high-end coaching program, Synchronize, was created along with an updated version of Sales Camp. It was pretty wild changing everything at the same time, but I could sense how these new classes would impact my clients! **The New Belief:** *We cannot create "the new" while we are holding on to "the old."*

Added 5 new people to my team (amazing support!). Building your team can be "challenging and expensive," which was my Limiting Belief at the time. You never know if someone is going to work out, even after you spend time and money training them. A well-known coach once said that you should build your team today for the company you want tomorrow. I took that advice and, in a leap of faith, brought on 5 new people. I didn't think I could afford them, but what was amazing was how quickly my revenue grew after I hired them! **The New Belief:** *Hiring a powerful team creates the bridge to the company we want tomorrow.*

Doubled my business—again. 2012 was a great year but 2013, 2014, and 2015 just kept getting better and better! I had an entirely new velocity with my new programs and teams. I kept raising our monthly revenue goals even though my old belief had been that I would have to work harder and longer. I knew better. I knew that we would be helping even more clients, so that overrode my old belief, and we kept meeting our new goals. My long-awaited goals of what was possible were coming true before my eyes. I remembered that Bob Proctor once said it was easier to make $50,000 per month than it was to make $50,000 per year, and I could now see that in action in my own business. The best part? I was spending more time at the spa and working much less. **The New Belief:** *Achieving sales goals is a direct reflection of how we are being in the world—when we are a confident leader, deliver products and services that solve our client's problems, and are committed to the success of our clients— anything is possible!*

Took a 12-day cruise through the Mediterranean (16 days off) with my husband and family (while I was 5 months pregnant)! We took a leap of faith and booked the cruise BEFORE I had the amazing team in place. Once the team was in place, though, I still knew it would be frightening to take 16 days away from my company and trust that everything would go smoothly. But it did! **The New Belief:** *We don't have to do it alone. There are talented people who can help us get things done faster and easier than if we try to do them! Plus, our company can grow faster!*

Received 5 separate awards for my books (Including an International Book Award and Beverly Hills Book Awards). My dear friend and business associate, Jenee Dana, encouraged me to enter my books into a few book contests. Of course, my Limiting Belief was, "What if they don't win? What if no one likes them?" Amazingly, the first two contests that I entered them in chose my books as winners and finalists! I'm so glad I took those steps. **The New Belief:** *Books are "Divine Downloads" to us and when we remember that they are gifts from God and our job is to get the messages out to the world, then we get out of their way and they take on a life of their own!*

Wrote and published my 2ᴺᴰ bestseller, *Selling With Synchronicity*. Having made *Selling With Intention* a bestseller, I decided that *Selling With Synchronicity* should also be a bestseller. Why not? Although I had some limiting thoughts like, "What if it doesn't happen again? What if I don't know what to do?" I trusted the process, got committed, and told everyone I knew that it was happening again. **The New Belief:** *When we know it really isn't about us, but about getting the message out to the masses, and focus on THAT, the rest is easy.*

Received a 5-star review on my novel and am finally publishing it! I wrote my novel alongside *Selling With Intention* because the process of writing creatively seemed to make it easier to write my non-fiction books. Lo and behold, I wrote an entire novel. I kept it a secret because my Limiting Belief was that writing a novel would distract from my business brand. **The New Belief:** *I realized that my brand isn't JUST about selling; it is also about creating a beautiful FULL life where we have enough money to give back to the organizations we care about AND live a great life.*

Had a baby. My husband and I wanted to start a family for a long time, but it didn't happen for us. In fact, at one point, we didn't believe that we could have biological children so we were contemplating the adoption process. And, I thought I was just "too old" anyway. And then one day, at the age of almost 39, I found out I was pregnant. What a surprise! **The New Belief:** *I let go of how our family would come to us, I just believed that it would happen.*

Shared the stage with Les Brown. I've always wanted to share the stage with Les Brown, but I had a Limiting Belief that said, "That will never happen because you will never be at his level." I know I wrote it down somewhere along the line and then it happened. The amazing part was that I followed HIM on stage and managed to keep the attention of the audience! **The New Belief:** *I had to believe that I belonged on the same stage as Les Brown.*

Experienced more peace, joy, and bliss than I've ever experienced. My husband comments on this frequently. He keeps saying he's never seen me so peaceful. For a long time, I didn't think I could have a successful business, a family, and feel peaceful all at the same time. I thought that a combination like that would require a feeling of chaos. But that just wasn't true. I think my peaceful state is a combination of many things, but mostly the result of my commitment to a life of dreaming, committing, and creating—and knowing that anything is possible! **The New Belief:** *I had to believe that a life of dreaming, committing, and creating anything is more than possible, and keep the faith that everything was unfolding perfectly—no matter what showed up.*

Purchased a Lake Home with a million-dollar view. The original goal was to purchase a property with an ocean view.

The truth is, we already own a property with an ocean view; we just haven't built on it yet. But we are water babies, so that goal morphed into living by a lake with a million-dollar view. But after all of our losses in real estate, we didn't think we would ever be able to qualify or have the money to purchase our dream property. But we wrote it on the checklist anyway and, voila, the Lake Home appeared! **The New Belief:** *I had to believe that purchasing a lake home with a million-dollar view was just as easy as purchasing a home without a lake view. And, it really was!*

Are you getting inspired yet? I hope so! This is just the beginning for you to see what's REALLY possible for you. It took years for me to get to the point where creating whatever I wanted, almost like having a magic wand in my hand, got easy. By reading this book, you will save yourself from having to read the hundreds of books and attend the hundreds of seminars that I have attended. I will fast-track you to the world you've been dreaming of.

THE BELIEF ZONE

"If I have the belief that I can do it, I shall surely acquire the capacity to do it even if I may not have it at the beginning."

~Mahatma Ghandi ~

I REMEMBER SITTING IN THE middle of my kitchen floor, looking at a pile of bills (mostly credit cards and real estate bills) and feeling a tremendous foreboding in the pit of my stomach.

How are we going to pay all of them? What is going to happen to us?

I had lots of questions but no answers. Tears were running down my face as I felt all of our dreams washing away down some unnamed sewer drain.

The dark thoughts started to swirl up even though I fought hard against them. Going against everything I had learned—everything I knew—I could hear the thoughts berating me, "This is what you get for taking so many risks. This is what you get for believing all of those stupid Law of Attraction books. This is what you get for thinking you'd figured it all out."

I had read so many books on The Law of Attraction, Manifesting Money, Attracting Abundance, Quantum Physics, and more. And yet, here I was, sitting on the cold tile, listening to that voice, feeling like my life was over.

And whose voice was that, anyway?

As the dark thoughts swirled about losing so much money, watching our real estate portfolio crumble, and potentially losing everything, there was another thought that hurt even more, lurking below all of it. And that thought was, *"You are getting too old to have kids. Plus, you couldn't even afford them at this rate. You better let that dream go too."*

I stared at my cat, Joe, and he stared back at me with that puzzled look that cats get when they are trying to figure out whether or not they can understand the words you are saying.

But Joe finally walked away because he got tired of trying to listen.

To be honest, I was tired of listening to myself! The self-pity had become tiresome. But the negative thoughts just kept ripping through my mind. I knew that the negative thoughts were keeping me stuck right where I was, but I didn't know what I could do to change them.

It was like a record had gotten stuck and just kept playing—over and over again—the same words: *"All of your dreams and goals are gone. The only thing you can do right now is try to clean this big mess up."*

Wait a second! With all of my training and experiences with clients, if there is anything that I know, it is that THIS kind of thinking is not going to get me out of my mess... it is just going to take me deeper.

And then I got on my knees and I started to pray.

In that moment of pain, in the middle of my prayer, I made a decision, which was more impactful than I could have imagined.

I am going to apply everything I have learned in the area of creation and manifestation so that we (my husband and I) can move out of these financial challenges back to a place of ease, grace, and cash flow. God, please help me. I commit to sharing this with anyone and everyone who will listen.

And then I felt a great peace wash over me.

As difficult as it was coming out of that dark moment, I started to choose new thoughts. Thoughts that would begin to move me in the right direction—the direction that I actually wanted to go. Thoughts that would take me out of this painful Comfort Zone I had created.

EVERYONE STARTS (AND RESTARTS) SOMEWHERE

I wrote this book for you—the seeker. The one who has been studying the Law of Attraction, metaphysics, Quantum Physics, or just Achievement in whatever fashion it showed up for you. And yet, no matter how many books you have read, seminars you've attended, or attempts you've made, you haven't reached your sales goals...or your other goals for that matter. You're stuck. You keep working really hard and getting the same results. If you are feeling like you are in a deep mess, there is a way out. I assure you, I have been to some of those deep dark places and I have found my way, and you can too. It begins now, in your mind.

Or maybe you have reached some goals and experienced a Quantum Leap or two, but you cannot figure out how to do it again—how to repeat it...and hopefully STAY IN THE FLOW.

For you, the purpose of this book is to give you a repeatable process—a blueprint for creation— that shows you WHY you could achieve that success before and, hopefully, which steps you've been missing as you've been working toward your new goals. It also provides a stopgap, so that you can have a moment before your thoughts take you in a direction you don't want.

The Belief Zone Blueprint that I am going to share with you has worked for me, my clients, and my readers who were brave enough to take another shot at their greatest dreams. Brave enough to step out of their safest Comfort Zone. I'm not special. In fact, if you ever met me, you will find that I am a down-to-earth farm girl from Minnesota. I'm not a quantum physicist but I am a seeker. And because of the hundreds of books I have read and the hundreds of thousands of dollars I have paid to be mentored and coached by some of the most successful people in the self-help industry, I do believe I have something to share with you. Something that is sure to change your life as much as it's changed mine—if you let it.

Ready to figure out how?

Well, first a word of warning. As we move down this path, the most important thing you can do is not give up. Sometimes things might not look like they are changing, but they really are. Sometimes it might feel like you are even taking a giant step back, but you might not be. Instead, recognize that as long as you continue to do this "work," you will begin to receive signs that, indeed, your dreams and goals are on their way.

You can launch that business or take that new outside sales job. Your sales really can go up. Hey, they might even double. You can grow your team. Buy that house. Grow your family. Decide to only work with your top 20% of prospects. Whatever the dream is, it's possible!

Now, we're ready to begin!

THE POWER OF BELIEF

First of all, never underestimate the power of our beliefs on our ultimate success, and I'm talking about our positive beliefs as well as our negative beliefs. In fact, our negative beliefs are probably the most impactful when we give them more "play time" than our positive beliefs. And, I understand that it can be easier to give them more "play" when we are on a downward spiral and everything seems to be falling apart, but we don't have to.

That's right. You can choose new thoughts.

Your beliefs hold your subconscious programming together and impact every thought you have, expectation you hold, decision you make, and action you take. If you want to have different results, you must begin at the basic level of beliefs—for the purposes of this book—about money, sales, business, yourself, and more. Remember, your beliefs affect your thoughts, how you feel, and ultimately what you attract into your reality.

Can you think of a time when you expected something to happen and it didn't? How did you feel? Probably not great. Do you remember some of the Limiting Beliefs or thoughts you might have had regarding it not being possible?

At the same time, can you think of a time when you expected something to happen, and it did—exactly as you had hoped? Think back to that moment to remember how great it actually felt! And what I really want you to notice is how your *expectation* about what was going to happen impacted your actual creation.

A client recently shared with me how powerful her expectations were on an ultimate result that she achieved. And believe me, this was no small feat, as she had accomplished an incredible goal. She held onto her positive belief for months and then, out of the blue, she found out that she had won an incredible contest—and yet, she wasn't surprised. I asked her why she wasn't surprised and she replied, "Because I knew that I was going to win that opportunity." She just knew. She expected it to happen.

Random House dictionary defines *expectation* as *"a prospect of future good or profit."* When you "just know," it's amazing what can happen.

Later, she was working on another large client opportunity but had some fear around whether or not it would happen. She was preparing for the client meeting the next day and I asked her, "Remember how you felt when you won that incredible contest?"

She thought for a moment and then said, "Yes, I remember."

"That's the same feeling and expectation that I want you to take into this client appointment."

"Okay! I got it!" and she took that feeling and expectation with her to the prospect meeting.

And guess what? She landed the deal! And went on to create another successful business.

But how can YOU get to that point of "just knowing"?

That's what this book is about. It's about helping you get into The Belief Zone where you can expect great things to happen to you.

LIMITING BELIEFS VS. ACHIEVING BELIEFS

We hear a lot about Limiting Beliefs, but what are they really? A *Limiting Belief* is a belief that hinders your success and forward movement in any way and prevents you from achieving the success you desire. It's also a belief that really isn't true when you look more closely. A Limiting Belief keeps you stuck somewhere in your business or in your life and limits your success. It keeps you trapped in your Comfort Zone.

An *Achieving Belief*, on the other hand, as defined in my other book *One Great Goal*, is a belief that supports your overall goals and is in alignment with your values and your purpose.

So when can you change a Limiting Belief? Now—in the moment that you need to change it. If a belief is just a "thought you think is true," as Jerry and Esther Hicks say, you can change it anytime. You can also change it when you realize it is inhibiting your success, when you notice that you aren't achieving the goals you desire, and when you feel blocked.

A question I get asked a lot is, "Are beliefs more than positive thinking?" Yes, because beliefs are just old thoughts that you believe are true (that you might not even be aware of). You can be a positive thinker and still have Limiting Beliefs running your show, stopping you from getting what you want. I'm not saying positive thinking is bad, at all. I think it's important to manage your thoughts, but it's easy to lie to yourself with surface positive thinking that doesn't go deeper into the underlying beliefs. One of my favorite books is the *Power of Positive Thinking* by Norman Vincent Peale because it is more than just positive thinking—it's about changing the way you think, letting go of worry, reaching your goals, and more. His book is full of gems that have helped generations of people change their lives.

So where are these Limiting Beliefs lurking? This question plagued me throughout my undergraduate degree in Psychology, during my NLP Training, and as I was getting my Master's Degree in Counseling Psychology. According to the research, Limiting Beliefs are swimming around in our subconscious mind. The concept of the subconscious mind was introduced near the beginning of the 20th century by psychologists, the most famous being Sigmund Freud. He speculated that it was a very dark place where repressed desires live.

Carl Jung came along, disputing that and suggesting that the subconscious was actually the collective unconscious mind, and that we could actually tap into a greater consciousness at any time. He was basically saying that we could tap into our individual consciousness as well as the collective unconsciousness of everyone on the planet. Yes, we could access all of the answers to our questions by tuning into, and downloading, all of the thoughts that are "floating" out there. All of the great ideas and inventions, in his opinion, came from the collective consciousness. In his theory, our personal consciousness holds our beliefs while the collective unconscious holds the beliefs and knowledge of all, including a higher power, that we can tap into any time we need it.

I think Carl Jung was on to something that hasn't been explored enough. We all have those moments where we receive what I like to think of as a "Divine Download," or those ideas that just seem to pop into our minds out of nowhere. Where do those ideas come from? I believe books, music, art and all great works are coming from the collective unconscious, which is why publishing companies often get very similar manuscripts and proposals at the same time. So then the question is: "Can we tap into the collective unconscious?" I believe that we can and that we do it whenever we are fully engulfed in our passion and doing what we love. You've felt those moments when you feel in the flow and everything just seems to get done quickly and easily, right? Those are the moments that you are tapped into the collective unconscious.

To take that idea even further, it may be possible to tap into the (achieving) collective unconscious beliefs that exist in the world. For example, if you want to bring more money into your life, then tapping into other people's beliefs around the area of money can be extremely powerful. If this seems like a stretch, it could be as simple as imagining what you think someone with a rich money mindset might believe about earning, spending, and saving money. If you don't know, pick up some books of wealthy people that you admire and step into their thoughts and beliefs to notice how they think differently. Or imagine yourself as that millionaire or billionaire that you desire to be. How different would your decisions be if they were made from these bigger beliefs?

EXPECTATIONS AND BELIEFS IN SALES AND INCOME GROWTH

So what is a belief? As I mentioned earlier, my favorite explanation is by Jerry and Esther Hicks in their book, *The Law of Attraction.* They state that beliefs are just thoughts we think are true. That's it. (I'm a big fan of simplifying things!) They are habitual thoughts that we just keep regurgitating in our brains over and over again and keep "believing them true." Believing them into our reality, into our existence. Makes sense, doesn't it?

Greg Kuhn, in his book *Why Quantum Physicists Do Not Fail* writes, "I have explained, of course, that your beliefs create your expectations, and that your expectations create your physical experiences. Your beliefs are powerful and necessary things for the human experience. They are the internal 'drivers' of your expectations that you will now learn to change and, when changed, will create a new universe for you to see."

So if our expectations really do impact our beliefs, why don't we pay more attention to them? In my experience, having coached hundreds of entrepreneurs and sales professionals over the years, it's because we just aren't aware. We don't pay attention to our beliefs and expectations on a regular basis, or even have the slightest understanding of how they directly impact our reality because we are on autopilot. Some people describe it as Level 1 Thinking, where we are just driven by our daily habits and routines—not by our true desires. We don't pay attention to where our expectations are pointing us because of those beliefs underneath, or what we are creating in our reality next. Instead, we just keep running from one thing to the next in our lives, never stopping to analyze what's working, what's not working, or what we really want next. We are socialized to do it once a year, at the beginning of a brand new year, but it's not enough to attain the lasting results we desire.

Even more, our beliefs directly impact the intentions and goals we choose from the beginning. Think about that for a minute. If we don't believe something is possible, and no one ever challenges that belief, then we can't choose a powerful belief or expectation that will actually take us to the next level. For example, think of someone who has always gotten C's in school. If no one ever tells them that they can get an A, or no one ever coaches them on how to do that, it's unlikely they will ever get an A. They don't believe it is possible. However, numerous studies have been done to show that when teachers believe in their students and expect them to do well, the students do better and even excel. When someone else believes in us, we just might begin to believe what they see in us as well. I read a story once about a man who was told he was "slow" by his teacher because he had a difficult time learning how to read. As he continued on in school, he received terrible grades and eventually took a job as a factory worker. At the factory, he desired a new and more difficult job, which required that he take a test. Unbeknownst to him, it was an IQ test. It turned out he was actually a genius. He promptly quit his job, started his own company, and went on to become a multi-millionaire who launched multiple companies because he suddenly believed he was intelligent.

Are you curious about your beliefs and expectations and how they are impacting your ultimate success at this very moment? The simple way to discover how they are impacting your success is to think about your Sales Stretch Goal or the highest income goal you can imagine. A Sales Stretch Goal is a sales goal that feels like a stretch to you but is still *believable* at some level. When you think about your Sales Stretch Goal, or just think how much money you desire to make, what thoughts come up for you? What do you believe about that goal? Do you expect it to happen? Again, just notice your answers to these questions and you can quickly see what your beliefs are in this area and how they might be affecting your ultimate results.

For example, perhaps you've been averaging $40,000 per month in your sales and you'd like to get to $80,000 per month. When you check in with yourself, you realize that your beliefs are: 1. I don't know where I would find these clients, and 2. I don't believe that there are enough clients out there. Bingo!

Notice that if those are your beliefs and expectations, there's no way you are going to reach that stretch goal. It's a big red flag to show you that's it time to check on your beliefs and expectations and get them into alignment with your stretch goals. And this exercise is the same if you've been averaging $83,000 per month and want to get to $166,000 per month (or from $1 million dollars in annual revenue to $2 million dollars in annual revenue).

How do you do that?

Well, there are a few steps you have to take before you change a belief for long-lasting results, but that's what this book is all about. So keep reading!

BELIEF + QUANTUM PHYSICS > THE BELIEF ZONE

I was in the middle of an interview with Greg Kuhn, author of the bestselling series *Why Quantum Physicists*, talking about the practical application of Quantum Physics, when he said something so profound to me that it stopped me in my tracks: "Ursula, we may not be quantum physicists, but that doesn't mean we don't have an important role to play. What we are demonstrating is the practical application of Quantum Physics on things like life and sales."

I remember making him stop for a moment because it was as if a lightning bold had struck me in the head. Greg was so right. I'd always questioned myself—whether or not I should even be talking about Quantum Physics because I didn't feel qualified. However, in that moment, I realized that I was more than qualified to *apply everything* I was learning about Quantum Physics to sales and goal achievement, so I could *share everything* I was learning with my clients to help them realize their goals.

Deep down, I knew this is one of the reasons I am on the planet. Again, one of those "obvious" moments when I was reminded that this is part of my journey and it doesn't really matter if I think I am "qualified." That 'qualified' belief can be limiting and tricky!

I believe that each and every one of us has a Comfort Zone that we are currently living in. But it's not The Belief Zone that we would like to be living in.

Random House Dictionary defines a *belief* as, *"something* *believed; an opinion or conviction: a belief that the earth is flat; confidence in the truth or existence of something not immediately susceptible to rigorous proof: a statement unworthy of belief; confidence; faith; trust: a child's belief in his parents; a religious tenet or tenets; religious* creed *or faith: the Christian belief."* The sentence that strikes me is, *"the truth or existence of something not immediately susceptible to rigorous proof."*

In The Belief Zone, we have beliefs that we currently hold true as an "opinion or conviction"—things that we "just know" are true. Then, there are those beliefs we wish were true that aren't currently in our Comfort Zone. Our intention, then, becomes to bring those beliefs that we desire into our New Belief Zone.

Random House dictionary defines a *zone* as, *"any continuous tract or area that differs in some respect, or is distinguished for some purpose, from adjoining tracts or areas, or within* which *certain distinctive circumstances exist or are established."*

Here's an easy way to think about it: Your Comfort Zone is actually a deflective energetic shield because the thoughts, emotions, and beliefs you currently have shield you from what you really want. You actually repel your desires and goals because the thoughts, beliefs, and emotions of your Comfort Zone aren't in alignment with them. So your New Belief Zone is an upgraded energy field that contains the thoughts, beliefs, and emotions that ARE in alignment with your deepest desires. When you enter a New Belief Zone, your energy field and frequency amp up and expand—essentially attracting and allowing in what you are willing to receive.

Consider this, what if you could create a powerful New Belief Zone that would allow you to create your deepest desires? What if that Belief Zone tapped into the universal knowledge that exists around us so that you could reach your financial goals, give back to the organizations you care about, AND live an authentic life?

When I was working on this book, I shared the ideas with anyone who would listen. One day, I shared it with a gentleman from one of my event sponsors. Thomas looked at me and said, "That's it! I always wondered where I went after I left my Comfort Zone! Now I know!" Bingo. Your Belief Zone.

The Belief Zone is just that—a place where *"certain distinctive circumstances exist or are established."* Most of us will benefit from establishing a New Belief Zone, as it is probable that the one we have isn't really working as well as we'd like it to. There are those lucky folks, though, who seem to be born into an already powerful Belief Zone. You know who I am talking about. Those interesting individuals who are born into a family situation where it just seems like their Belief Zone Blueprint (more on that later) is automatically programmed for wealth and good fortune. In fact, it's as if they never have to think about creating wealth or good fortune—they just expect it, *and so it is.* Think of a wealthy family that you admire in your community. Why do you admire them? Think about their children. Notice how their expectations about life may have been different than yours. Also, notice the doors that those expectations opened up for their children. Maybe Ivy League schools. Maybe a different standard of living than yours. We can judge them and feel a level of envy, or we can learn from their expectation that they deserved great things in life because that is what they were taught.

Think about that for a moment. Again, you might have even been envious of these individuals at one time or another, but the truth is they don't know the difference. They don't understand a life *without* wealth or good fortune; *it just is.* Does that mean their life is "perfect"? Again, that's up to interpretation, but we often hear of people who seem to have everything handed to them financially but then struggle in other areas of their life. So the ideal Belief Zone Blueprint would include all of these areas: Wealth, Health, Relationships, Spiritual or Religious, etc. and not necessarily in that order.

QUANTUM PHYSICS AND SPIRITUALITY

In his book *Infinite Potential*, Lothar Schäfer considers whether or not Quantum Physics and spirituality are interconnected: "Physicists typically believe that their experiments have forced them to develop the concepts of quantum theory. Out of the experiments with elementary particles, atoms, and molecules, all these unexpected ideas arose of wave functions, quantum numbers, and so on. In reality, practically all of the unexpected concepts that quantum physicists are using to describe the world were invented by spiritual teachers thousands of years ago. The quantum numbers, the concept of potentiality, the principle of wholeness, the importance of waves as the source of the manifested world—all of these ideas have historically spiritual roots. Does that make Quantum Physics a kind of spirituality?" And he goes on to say, "Physicists don't have spiritual issues in mind when they design their experiments, and they shouldn't. At the same time, once they have put their findings out to the world, the findings are out of their hands, and they shouldn't forbid anyone to draw their conclusions."

That's exactly it. The scientific community is doing their part to discover how things work, which is obviously helpful to furthering our knowledge of the universe. However, what we need to understand is practical application. What do their findings really mean to the humans on this planet? What should we be able to do once we understand this information and begin to apply it?

Kuhn and Schäfer remind us that it is everyone's responsibility to experiment and apply what the scientific community is showing us so that we can implement those teachings into our daily lives...and live better.

Let's imagine for a moment a world where every individual *believes* in their own potential and they don't have any fear or Limiting Beliefs about achieving the goals they desire. Let's imagine a world where people realize that they can find their way out of their current—and probably painful—situation through the power of their thoughts, beliefs, expectations, and actions. Imagine a world where people can live in their purpose and allow their path to unfold every day, magically, before them, unencumbered by the Limiting Beliefs and thoughts of others, effectively creating a new frequency that is open to receiving their hearts' desires. What would that world be like?

It would be an extraordinary world, and it's one that I love to co-create with you.

Does it mean that it would be perfect? No, far from it. Well, I should restate that—I guess it depends on what your beliefs are about perfection! Living on planet earth, we would still have loss and perceived pain, but we could certainly choose how we want to react to that and what we want to do next. I believe we can choose how we want to react to life and work on ourselves, and our expectations, regarding what we want to create.

I often think of Eliezer "Elie" Wiesel and what he shared in his book, *Night*. The man experienced unspeakable horrors in a concentration camp at the hands of the Nazis because of his religious beliefs. During much of his time there, he cried out to God and asked, "Why?" and "Where are you?" but didn't receive any answers. And through the silence and the "non-answers," he made a decision. He decided that no matter what, the one thing that the Nazis could not take from him was how he *reacted* to the situation. No one could take away his spirit. And I truly believe that the way he reacted to the situation is the reason he survived when so many others gave up their battle. He went on to write 57 books, become a professor and a political activist, and ultimately win the Nobel Peace Prize for his focus on teaching others to never forget or repeat the atrocities.

If Elie Wiesel can handle himself with such dignity in spite of unspeakable horrors, then why can't we choose to reframe how we see our pain and our challenges? Can we take a lesson from him that in spite of the pain we might face, we might rise above it anyway and make different decisions about how we will face the world—how we will react to what is thrown at us—

and ultimately what we will believe? Can we experience pain and still believe that the miracles we dream of are more than possible?

I believe we can. Yes, yes, we can.

I have read almost all of Jerry and Esther Hicks' books (better known as Abraham) from *The Law of Attraction* to *The Vortex*. They dig deep into the power of our beliefs and the impact belief has on the results we experience in life. As I mentioned before, I love how they define "belief" as a "thought we think is true," or in other words, a habitual thought that we almost become addicted to and continue to show ourselves and the rest of the world that it's true. And, well, the belief is true to us but it might not really be *true*. But how can that be?

What their books teach us is that the world is full of contrast. In other words, if we didn't have pain, we wouldn't understand joy. We wouldn't appreciate the "little things." If you've studied the laws of the Universe, you know that the Law of Polarity shows us that for every painful situation we are in, the exact opposite exists. For example, if you are in financial dire straits in your reality, the exact opposite financial reality also exists. Yes, the potential for you to be in full abundance exists at the exact same time. Think about that!

I've experienced the Law of Polarity (we all have), especially as it relates to our financial situation! When I finally "got this" Law of Polarity, my entire financial situation just flipped. I no longer struggled because my belief changed to what is possible in sales and finances—not "what was" in that moment, but the abundance that existed as the polar opposite of what I was experiencing at the time. And that belief allowed me to expect that my financial situation was about to change. And it did, one moment at a time.

THE CHOICE IS YOURS

So why doesn't this work for everyone? If Quantum Physicists are right about matter and the way we can influence our reality with our thoughts and emotions, then why aren't we all rich? Why aren't we all experiencing instant creations of our dreams and goals?

Because most of us aren't willing to study this "stuff," apply it to our own lives, and then take action. And, we give up way too soon—usually right before our goal is about to come into reality. Most of the world is drowning in confusion, fear, self-pity, sadness, envy, anger, and jealousy because they don't believe they can have what they really want. Plus, they are missing out on the practical application. As I've mentioned, I've literally read hundreds (maybe thousands) of books now on the topics of Quantum Physics, metaphysis, Law of Attraction, laws of the universe, sales, goal achievement etc. I've heard hundreds of different perspectives on what works and what doesn't work, and my intention in this book is to show you (from my experience) what really works in terms of changing your beliefs so you can change your ultimate results. I can show you real world examples of what has shown up in my life, and the lives of my clients, that will blow your mind—because it still blows my mind.

You might be thinking right now, *"That's great that it worked for you, Ursula, but I already know (a belief!) that it won't work for me."* I'll tell you right now, that's a load of you know what! It's an excuse and a decision to stay exactly where you are and to continue to accept a mediocre life. It's your decision, of course, but I beg you to consider something greater—to recognize that your Comfort Zone is just trying to keep you safe by keeping you exactly where you are.

I could show you the methodologies that I know really work, and sadly, you might still choose to live in a world that only holds pain and self-sabotage. Or, you could decide right now, in this moment, that you are done living like that. You are done with mediocrity and lowered expectations of what's possible. You are done with letting yourself off the hook every time you decide to make your life better and then give up. You are done with believing that success is for everyone else. And you are *ready* to do whatever it takes to change your beliefs and expectations into powerful possibilities for your sales results and ultimately your life.

But let me warn you. If it were "easy" to create a New Belief Zone (although you are welcome to change your belief to "easy" right now), everyone would be willing to do it. The truth is, most people are so entrenched in their negative habits of thinking, and self-sabotage, that they don't even open themselves up to new possibilities. They don't really want to change because it is more comfortable to stay exactly where they are. Don't be one of them. I beg you. Please, please, please don't be one of them. Choose to do the "work" now so that ease and flow can become your new conversation.

Your new way of life.

GETTING INTO THE BELIEF ZONE

Congratulations, you are still reading—you are still with me! You are now part of a very small percentage of people on this planet who are willing to become aware of their thoughts, beliefs, expectations, and ultimate actions so they can begin to change them. Statistically, I've read that only 3% of people regularly read books and attend training seminars. You are now part of that 3%.

Getting into a New Belief Zone is a choice. A choice to change. A choice to choose something new. You can choose to stay exactly where you are in your sales, business, and life, or you can *decide* to move beyond that and into what you know is really possible for you.

In the beginning, you will spend more time inside of your old Comfort Zone than in your New Belief Zone, but that's okay. I will give you tools and strategies you can use to spend more time in your New Belief Zone in The Belief Zone Blueprint section.

You will know when you are in your *chosen* New Belief Zone because everything will seem to flow effortlessly for you. You will experience instant creation in real time. For example, you might think about a potential new client and then, almost magically, you receive an email from them telling you that they are ready to purchase your new product or service. Or you might decide to hire a new sales person and then they *synchronistically* show up through someone you know. Coincidence will begin to seem like an everyday occurrence and you won't be able to deny all of the synchronicities that are showing up around you. Events will just begin to unfold the way you've been wanting them to and you will feel light, joyful, and excited about how things are just coming so easily!

I distinctly remember coming out of the Great Recession, after we had made the decision to turn everything around, when we received an unbelievable call. A miracle came out of the blue. I know these seemingly magical occurrences were due to being in our New Belief Zone and the new decisions we had made. We received a call from the loan holder of some land we owned on the West Coast. The company was going through a difficult time as well and had also been impacted by the Great Recession. Although we still owed almost $20,000 on the property, the company offered to settle with us for just $1,000. So we paid them the $1,000 they asked for and suddenly owned the land outright.

SUPPORTING YOUR NEW BELIEF ZONE

Mastering the creation of your New Belief Zone is the best place to begin because you can practice in small ways first to see how it works for you.

For example, you can set some mini-goals around things like winning a prize in a drawing or landing a new amazing client. Once that begins to feel easy for you, you can then expand into the area of sales, money, business success, and more. Clarity is where it all begins and it's where you will begin when you work on your own Belief Zone Blueprint.

A great place to "practice" your New Belief Zone is in the area of sales or your finances. Setting a sales goal that is a stretch but still believable to you is key. Remember, if you don't believe it at some level, it will be difficult for you to expect it to happen.

In the beginning, you might not entirely believe your new sales stretch goal is possible. In that case, I recommend that you reach out to someone who can hold that belief with you—a coach, mentor, friend, etc. Whoever it is, though, you must fully trust that they will hold your belief with you in a powerful way. If they have doubt, that will just reinforce your doubt. That's why I highly recommend hiring a professional coach to help you hold that space instead of a friend or mentor. A professional coach who has experienced tangible results with their clients already knows how to powerfully hold that space for you, and they can hold that space for you until you reach your goal. Also note that if you hire a coach, hire one who is ahead of you, who has already achieved the results that you desire.

In my own business, I have hired many successful coaches who are where I want to be in my own business in terms of their revenue and sales. When you hire a coach who is more successful than you are in terms of your sales results, not only can they hold that new belief with you, they can actually pull you energetically to that New Belief Zone. That's the best way for me to explain it. It's almost like their belief in you overrides your Limiting Beliefs until you get there. I do that for my clients all of the time (hold the beliefs for them) and it's powerful to be on both sides of it. I am always amazed by the results they receive!

One of my clients, Patti, had this exact experience. She really wanted to attend our two-day Sales Camp course but didn't have the funds at the time. In fact, she'd just gone through some significant personal challenges in her life and her savings and credit cards were wiped out. And yet, I had an intuitive feeling that money was trying to get to Patti (it's really always trying to get to everyone, but we block it) and I thought I could help her pretty quickly. I offered her a FREE 30 minute Sales Strategy Session to help her unlock where she was stuck. As a coach, when I offer FREE sales strategy session, I come from a place of detachment. My intention is to help first and to also make sure that Sales Camp is a fit for the individual, or I may need to refer them to someone else. In Patti's case, she was an excellent fit for Sales Camp and I told her that when she was ready and the money was flowing it, that we'd love to have her.

A few days later, I received an email from Patti with an unsolicited testimonial that she wanted me to have:

"Before working with Ursula, I was struggling with making enough sales to meet my monthly obligations. After working with Ursula for just 30 minutes, she helped shift my mindset from one of surviving to one of thriving, and provided me with sales strategies that catapulted me forward! The result? I made a single $6,000 sale the very next day with great ease, and secured a second 5-figure commitment from another client. Ursula's strategies work! Get yourself to her next Sales Camp and thrive!" Patti Cotton, MA, MAOD, PCC, executive coach and consultant, Patti Cotton, MA, MAOD, PCC

In just 30 minutes, Patti was able to shift her old "stuck" Comfort Zone into a New Belief Zone that allowed her to easily receive the money that was right there—the sales that were trying to get to her. In Patti's case, she had to believe that she deserved to make over $100,000 per year. The following year, Patti did just that. In the first six months of the year after that, she made over $100,000 on her way to her next level of $200,000+. As we were in the final stages of editing, Patti shared this post in our Synchronize Facebook group: *"I'm beyond grateful and ecstatic to share that Ursula Mentjes has once again helped me to double my income in 2016! Celebrating tonight and grateful for her expert support and counsel. Truly, Ursula is a coach 'extraordinare'!"*

And the sales are trying to get to you, too. They are trying REALLY hard to get to you. I share that with my clients all of the time because it's true. Our natural state in this world is abundance, but our negative thoughts prevent the sales from easily flowing to us.

Stop for a moment and think about how you are blocking your own sales. What are you doing to stop them? You are doing something to sabotage your sales results and prevent them from getting to you, but what?

Is it fear? Limiting Beliefs? Your old Comfort Zone? Whatever it is, I am determined to help get you out. You are reading this book right now, in this moment, because it's time to make a change. It's not okay to continue to deal with mediocrity. That's over. You are also no longer allowed to talk about "the bad economy" or any other reasons you've come up with regarding why you aren't reaching your goals because those old thoughts hold your Comfort Zone together. It's time to embrace the abundance and infinite possibilities that are right there for you, trying to get to you. By the time you finish reading this book, you will know how to create your own New Belief Zone and keep expanding it like Patti did.

YOUR MISSION, SHOULD YOU CHOOSE TO ACCEPT IT

One point of clarity before we continue: Your current Belief Zone *is* your Comfort Zone. It's the place—a deflective energy shield—that your ego loves to stay in because it's a very safe place. You don't have to strive for clarity. You don't have to change. You don't have to commit to anything new. You just get to be. And while it's comfortable and safe, it's not where you should stay very long if you want to live the life you've been dreaming about.

Your Comfort Zone actually breeds mediocrity in your life. It's basic, it's boring, and you wouldn't be reading this book right now if it was a place you were supposed to live and stay. In fact, this is your wakeup call. This is the sign you've been waiting for. This is your message to get up and get out of your Comfort Zone before you become too entrenched.

Let's face it. You've been living in your Comfort Zone for a long time. It's not a bad place to live. In fact, it probably feels safe, comfortable, and kind of nice. A safe harbor. The only problem is, it's not getting you where you want to go. And deep down, you're tired of living in that place.

I get it. I've been there. And the truth is, we usually don't get out of our Comfort Zone until it simply becomes too painful or uncomfortable to stay there.

I've been there, too.

In the beginning, your Comfort Zone and your Belief Zone are the same size. Let's say they kind of overlap. As you shift your belief, your New Belief Zone outgrows your old Comfort Zone so that with the New Belief Zone, suddenly your Comfort Zone is inside of the New Belief Zone, so it suddenly feels comfortable to you. That's a mouthful, isn't it?

Let me explain in greater detail. We can use a sales goal as an example. (That's why you are here anyway, right?) In the beginning, your sales goal might be $20,000 per month. I'm imagining that you are able to reach that pretty easily, but it's not getting you where you want to go in terms of sales success. And then you decide that your new sales stretch goal is $40,000 per month, and you decide to double your sales. Excellent.

What needs to happen next? First, you have to get clear on what you want, then you need to change your Limiting Beliefs around that sales goal, and finally, you need to get committed to your new goal. Throughout this book, I will take you through each part of the process so you can create your own Belief Zone Blueprint, but for the sake of this example, I just want you to see how you need to have clarity before you can examine your beliefs. Only then you can change a Limiting Belief that is stopping you from having what you want as you then move into actually committing to your new goal—and what it will take to maintain that level of success and grow from there.

THE MONEY IS OUTSIDE OF YOUR COMFORT ZONE

I'm going to tell you something you probably already know, but I feel it needs to be stated: The money you desire, your sales and or financial stretch goals, are not in your current Comfort Zone. How do I know? Because if they were, you wouldn't be reading this book. In fact, all of the sales you desire, plus the other goals you've been dreaming about, are right outside of your Comfort Zone.

Where, then, are the sales that you desire?

They are in your New Belief Zone, just waiting for you to claim them!

Suspend your disbelief for a moment, and imagine that they are actually there waiting for you. Imagine what your business and your life will be like when you reach that goal. What will be different? How will you be different? How will you show up?

It is time to design your New Belief Zone.

CREATE YOUR NEW BELIEF ZONE

Okay, this is the part you've been waiting for and the section that I am most excited about writing! As I've mentioned many times, I have read countless books on manifesting goals and have been frustrated to the core, and ultimately figured it out for myself. I know, in my heart, that this can work for you, too, because I have seen it work for my clients over and over again. You can do this! And, yes, it helps if you actually believe that this can work for you. Or, suspend your disbelief for a bit and just imagine that it is all possible for you, and I will hold that New Belief Zone with you.

I have included Quantum Corners that showcase some of my clients' results in each chapter to strengthen your New Belief Zone regarding what is possible for you. When you see others achieving goals that you'd like to achieve, it makes it easier for YOU to achieve those goals. In our Synchronize Coaching program, we noticed very quickly that as some of our clients broke through their sales barriers, others in the program quickly followed—so much so that we no longer have a year-long program because that just prolonged the time it took for our clients to reach their sales stretch goals!

Every time I see this, I'm reminded of the story of Roger Bannister. Before Roger, no one had ever run a mile in less than four minutes. In 1954, Roger ran it in just 3:59, shattering the common belief that a human could not run a mile in four minutes or less. Of course, that record has been broken multiple times since. It's interesting to note that the first time he broke through, it was only by one second, yet since, it has been shattered by as much as seventeen seconds.

I also love to think about the multiple accounts of people bending spoons, using only their mind and their intention. What is really interesting is that most report they couldn't get their spoon to bend at first, but as soon as they witnessed someone else's spoon bending, their belief shifted and their spoon appeared to almost turn to liquid for a second and then bend. In other words, as soon as they took on someone else's experience and belief, their spoon bent, too.

After years of studying, experimenting, and practicing various techniques on my own, and then helping clients double and triple their sales and achieve other big life goals, I've discovered that there are 7 simple steps that you can take to move into a New Belief Zone and ultimately achieve your most desired goals.

I will tell you, it is much easier to work on one goal at a time, which was the focus in my book *One Great Goal*. As you develop your "muscle" in the area of goal achievement and practice, you will be able to take on more goals all at once. In the beginning though, if you take on more than one goal at a time, it may take longer. I often have fifty or more goals that I am working on at one time, but The Belief Zone Blueprint (we will get to that soon) allows me to do that. You will be able to do that too, with time and practice.

I'm going to share the steps with you in The Belief Zone Blueprint, so don't try this at home until you have the entire blueprint in front of you!

STEP #1: CLARIFY

"Your vision will become clear only when you look into your heart. Who looks outside, dreams. Who looks inside, awakens."

~ Carl Jung ~

TIM AND I HAD been living in California for about 8 years when an incident happened that planted a seed and catalyzed a process of clarifying a goal to move back to Minnesota.

We flew back to Minnesota for a family event and my mom and my brother, Ron, were going to pick us up at the airport. When Tim and I arrived, they weren't there. I picked up my phone to call my brother and saw that he'd left a voicemail. My heart stuttered when I heard his distressed voice. My mom hadn't arrived at their designated meeting space, and he was worried. (My brother never worries!)

Oh no! What happened to my mom? Is she okay?

I called my brother immediately and when he answered, he still sounded concerned. My heart dropped. Mom hadn't shown up. And she didn't have a cell phone yet.

We chatted for a moment, deciding that he would drive back to her house since she wasn't answering her home phone and I would call the Sheriff's department in case she had been in an accident.

A woman at the Sheriff's department picked up the phone, identified herself, and asked me how she could help.

"My mom was supposed to have arrived at her destination an hour ago, and we don't know where she is. Has there been an accident on highway 60 or on County Road 12 going out of town?"

She checked with her dispatchers and got back on the phone immediately, "Yes, there's been an accident on highway 60 and we have a patrol car heading there now."

My heart stopped.

Please, God, please let Mom be okay. I promise that I will do whatever you want me to do. I'll even move back to Minnesota.

Why did I say that at that moment? Because I know that my Mom had prayed every day since I left that we would move back. Sure, she wanted me to be successful, happy, and living my dream life. She knew that we loved California and all of our friends there. But moms want their kids close, so who could blame her?

The dispatcher took down my number and told me she would call if that accident involved my mom.

She didn't call.

But Ron finally did. It turned out that Mom was at the wrong gas station, not the one where they were supposed to meet. Little did I know that the "deal" I had made with God was the first step toward clarity.

Maybe I'm supposed to be in Minnesota? I do want to be closer to my family. It would be great to move back there and start a family, and raise them with the love and presence of our extended family. I also love what I have created here—a thriving business, a powerful community, and so much more.

I felt a very profound inner conflict. And yet the clarifying signs kept coming and coming.

Years later, when the Great Recession hit and Tim and I had just had a rough experience with getting out of a very expensive business transaction (where we lost about $100,000, and that's not including all of our real estate losses), we were aimlessly driving down the road when we hit a dead end. I looked up at the road sign in front of us. (I cannot make this stuff up!) "Minnesota Road." We looked at each other and burst out laughing. Is that a sign or what?

God was pointing, but we still weren't listening! It would take us four more painful years to listen and begin to use the same steps I used to grow my business in quantum leaps to create a successful move back to Minnesota.

THE LAW OF ATTRACTION AND
WHY IT DOESN'T ALWAYS WORK

The Law of Attraction (LOA) is the Universal Law that states "like attracts like." It has been talked about for hundreds (potentially thousands) of years in different ways. It became more popular in the positive thought movement in the early 1900's. Most recently, it became mainstream due to the bestselling book and movie *The Secret*. Oh, wait. In case you were under a rock, *The Secret* was a movie and later a book talking about the LOA.

Rhonda Byrne, the author, featured many thought leaders and self-help authors and speakers in the film. For several of them, the movie catapulted their careers all the way to Oprah.

Like many others, I had been writing and talking about it before it became a phenomenon because of the work

of Rhonda Byrne, but after *The Secret* came out, I was just as excited as everyone else to continue to apply the Law of Attraction. I had written *Selling With Intention*, and I had even talked about the LOA in my book. As I mentioned, people have been talking about the LOA for hundreds of years and in many different ways, so *The Secret* wasn't really a secret at all. However, Rhonda Byrne was one of the most talented marketing geniuses of all time and she brought the information and experts together in a powerful way and, I believe, helped a lot of people see that they had more control over their lives than they had ever imagined. It got people dreaming again.

As for me, *The Secret* motivated me to take more risks because I figured I could handle it, especially armed with confidence from the movie and all of the training I had under my belt. Tim and I purchased a lot of real estate and I purchased countless coaching programs and more, creating a tremendous amount of debt, which created even more pressure to write more books, grow my business, and take care of my clients. All self-imposed pressure, of course, but I was learning from all of these coaches and I had a list of things that I now HAD to do. To give myself credit, I was also selling a lot in my business and Tim was making a solid income as well. We just got a little—okay... a lot!—over-zealous on the risk-taking side.

If I would have stopped for a minute, I might have realized that all of the pressure I was putting on myself wasn't healthy and wasn't necessarily in my best interest or in the best interest of my business. It felt like there was a lot of good stuff happening, but also like I was forcing those things to happen. Even though I was using what I thought was the LOA, it still felt like I had to put a tremendous amount of effort into everything I was doing. At times, it felt like I was running through quicksand. I could see the goals right ahead of me, but I was going to have to work *really hard* to make them happen.

The good news is that LOA motivated me to get a lot of things done and to believe that they could happen. And a lot of things did happen. What I didn't realize then, though, was why certain things happened and others didn't. As I've shared in my books and at speaking engagements, and in The Belief Zone section in this book, my husband and I lost hundreds of thousands of dollars when the most recent recession hit. I know we weren't alone in that. I also know that I wouldn't have taken as many risks if it hadn't been for my belief in the LOA. And, unfortunately, that was how I learned that the LOA was only part of the strategy that I needed to create everything I wanted in my life. If Tim and I had understood the other Laws and the tools I've acquired to leverage them, which I'm going to share with you in this book, I don't think we would have lost as much money in the recession as we did. I also think my business would have grown with much less effort, like I experience now.

Let's also be clear that I was in a tremendous amount of resistance. I didn't want things to change. We had created an amazing life, while we accumulated a lot of debt; and when the great recession hit, we realized that our life was about to change quickly. But I resisted that change. I wasn't willing to receive the change that had to happen so we could clear out the "old" to make room for the "new." So, it took us a lot longer to get out of our (perceived) bad situation than it really needed to. One of the things I've learned about change is that you must be willing to receive all of it—the good and the bad—or you can't make room for all of the good that is coming to you.

Would I change what happened and what we lost? Absolutely not, because it gave me the real world experience to now help my clients in ways that I couldn't have before. Would I want to live it all over again? No way.

In my opinion, when the LOA doesn't work, it's because your belief system isn't consciously in alignment with your goal. And, quite possibly, you are choosing goals that aren't in alignment with your *values*. Which actually means that the LOA is actually always working, as it tunes into your Comfort Zone, your energy shield, and gives you what you are willing to receive.

There. I said it. And that's basically it. Simple to say... harder to change.

When your belief system and values are in alignment with your goals, the LOA works with amazing results. Things will flow more easily to you. You will be a powerful receiver. It's not that you won't put effort in or take inspired action, but you definitely won't feel like you are slogging through quicksand. I wrote a lot about that in *Selling With Synchronicity*, so definitely check out that book if you want to go deeper there.

But when you're not in alignment with your values and beliefs, the LOA can actually create a lot of mess, confusion, and disappointment. I was reading another book recently (yes, I read a lot) and the author was talking about the LOA. They gave a specific example of how someone they knew had attracted a very expensive car (let's say a Bentley) because they had it on their vision board and did whatever they needed to do to bring it into reality. And they did. That Bentley showed up. But it wasn't in alignment with their belief system (or their values, for that matter), so they couldn't afford the repairs and ultimately couldn't keep it.

Another example is lottery winners. We hear about lottery winners all of the time and how they ultimately can't hold on to their wealth. The money wasn't in alignment with their current belief system. Their subconscious belief might have been something like, "Rich people are greedy." And maybe they believed that if they were greedy, they would lose their family or friends, which shows where their value really is. So they had to get rid of the lottery winnings as fast as they could before that happened (all subconsciously, of course). If you have issues around self-worth and deserving, the first place it usually shows up is money, which is a great and painful way to figure out what's really going on.

YOU AND THE LAW OF ATTRACTION

Think about your own sales, business, and life. Are there times when you have attracted something and then it quickly disappeared? Maybe the LOA worked to help you get things but not keep them because you didn't know how to change your beliefs or whatever you thought you wanted to attract wasn't in alignment with your values.

More frequently, though, I work with people whose belief systems don't allow them to even attract the things they desire in the first place. In my work as a sales coach and sales trainer, the first place it often shows up is in sales. My clients want to attract more sales, but there seems to be something blocking them. They practice all of the strategies they've learned through the LOA, but it's not enough; and by the time they get to me, they are burned out and frustrated. What they don't realize is that they have subconscious beliefs confusing their Clarity.

That's why in all of the training I do (from Sales Camp to private Synchronize Sales coaching), I always begin with Clarity in the goals, values, and belief system. If I can figure out what you want and what you believe about sales, sales people, money and selling, I can usually help you create alignment between these and release the old beliefs and create new beliefs so you can achieve the sales goals you desire. Better yet, once you create the sales you desire, the money won't just disappear because you will have new beliefs in place and a plan for the money.

QUANTUM CORNER

PATTI COTTON

President & CEO, Cotton Group LLC

www.PattiCotton.com

WHEN I SIGNED UP for Sales Camp in late September, I had made just $6,000 that year. I had my pre-Sales Camp coaching call with Ursula and, after the call, went out and sold $30K worth of contracts even before Sales Camp began. At Sales Camp, I recognized the value of investing in Synchronize, signed up, and went on to make $100K that year. The following January, I already had contracts and commitments for $200K! And it's only January! When I decided to attend Sales Camp, I knew I needed clarity around my pricing and a strategic process for selling.

When I wrote down my one great goal of $100K, it was hard to imagine. But as I did my projections, I saw how it could happen. Doing these actually showed me I could do it successfully. The practices/beliefs that helped me the most include gratitude and the understanding that God wants abundance for me and that He asks me to share my gifts to make people's lives better. New habits that I created for myself included a lot more self-care. The more we dedicate our gifts to making the lives of others better, the more self-care we need to support that.

Before Sales Camp, I believed that sales was pushy,

disingenuous, self-serving. I actually wanted to hire a sales person since I didn't think I could do it well. My new belief that I created at Sales Camp was that sales *is* service and if I don't offer my services, I am withholding the answer that a lot of people need to make their lives better. That new belief allowed me to sell from the heart, to gain confidence, and to become excited about helping more people.

The three actions that I took that made the biggest impact in my sales were systematizing my sales process, refining my strategy conversation, and prioritizing my daily activities to do income-producing activities FIRST.

Now I KNOW that selling is simply presenting people with opportunity to make their lives better. Who wouldn't want to help others do that? Sales and selling can be fun, genuine, exciting, and rewarding.

As a result of moving into a New Belief Zone, I have gone from a stretch goal of $200K (which has been hard to believe in the past), to now contemplating creating a multi-million-dollar business that I can eventually sell. My stretch goal this year is $500K—and I am now putting together plans to make that happen.

CHOOSE CLARITY

Before you start creating your sales stretch goals or new income goals and a powerful life, get really clear on what that means to you. Really think about who you are—the whole of you—your values and purpose for being on this earth. Learn to discern between your own voice and the voice of others who "thought" they were helping you. Or the voice of others and what they told you to do. It's important to follow our own intuition and we know is right and will work best for us. It's about taking our full power back and taking full responsibility for everything that is in our lives, so we can create from a place of power. Question everything, for in those questions, you will begin to find your answers.

Imagine for a moment that you had a very magical wand that would allow you to create anything you wanted in your life, from health to wealth. Imagine that you were not limited in any way. Imagine that the first thought you had about what you wanted wasn't big enough and you could choose again—you could choose what you've been whispering to yourself inside, in terms of what you really want. Imagine that it could be that easy.

Let me guess? The moment I asked you to think about what you wanted to create, you started to think about what's not working in your life first, right? Maybe you immediately thought about the reasons why you could never get what you desire anyway. Notice how your ego can jump in really quickly and begin to self-sabotage your creative efforts.

I've always said that Clarity = Achievement. But you can't get to Clarity if you aren't willing to figure out what you don't want and then give yourself permission to dream. Maybe you even feel like your "magic wand" is broken because you haven't used it in a long time. That's okay, we can fix your wand. Again, gaining Clarity allows you to finally give yourself permission to have what you want. It then allows your Limiting Beliefs to show up so you can release them. And then, once you do, get ready because your commitment to your success will allow you to see the next steps that are right in front of you.

To help you with this process, I'd like you to think about what you don't want first. It's much easier to think about what you DO want when you have clarity on what you DON'T want.

For example, if you don't want to have any more debt, what you are really saying is that you want to be debt-free. To take it to an even more positive level, what you really want is to have all of your debts paid in full and have money in the bank.

What else are you "done with" in your life that you just want to let go of? Take a moment to write those things down.

START WITH WHAT YOU DON'T WANT

Again, begin by writing down all of the goals that you know you *don't* want in life. Perhaps these were goals that you had in the past. Maybe you thought you wanted to be a lawyer and then later changed your mind. You would write "lawyer" because you absolutely now know that you don't want to do that. There could also be other things like "stress" that are less tangible. Doesn't it feel good to write down all of those things that you are sure you don't want to do anymore? You are on your way to clarity!

MY LIST OF WHAT I KNOW I DON'T WANT IN MY LIFE:

1. To become a lawyer

2. To work for less than I am worth

3. To work for someone else

4. To work so hard and often that it impacts my health

5. To lose sight of what is most important

6. To feel like work is "work"

7. To feel stressed all of the time

8. To feel like what I am doing doesn't have any purpose

9. To do something that doesn't directly impact the lives of others

YOUR LIST OF WHAT YOU KNOW YOU DON'T WANT IN YOUR LIFE:

1. _____
2. _____
3. _____
4. _____
5. _____
6. _____
7. _____
8. _____
9. _____
10. _____
11. _____
12. _____
13. _____
14. _____
15. _____

Now, let's get back to what you DO want. Often, those things are the opposite of the items you've just listed. See how easy that is?

Close your eyes for a moment and really go there. Imagine that you have created this dream in real life. Be there in that visualization, fully there in the moment. What do you see around you? Who is in the visualization with you? What have you created? How much money are you making? What's going on in your life? Who are you in relationships with? Now, step into this fully. You are no longer viewing yourself in this space, you are actually there, in the moment. Notice the colors that you see around you. Notice the scents that you smell. Even more importantly, notice what it feels like inside to create this goal. Whatever that feeling is, I want you to multiply it by ten and allow it to reach way out in the world. Revel in that moment. Revel in that feeling. And know that everything that you saw in that visualization, everything you desire in your life, is waiting for you to let it in.

So, what do YOU want to create in the next 12 months? In my second book, *One Great Goal*, I discovered an easy way to figure out what you really want by discovering your most desired goal. There is so much power in figuring out what your heart and Soul is really calling out for. Once you know that, the "how" to get there becomes clear really fast.

STAY FOCUSED ON YOUR SOUL PURPOSE

Take a moment and just begin to write down all of the things you want, but first…anchor into your Soul Purpose, so that your Soul and Sole Purpose become the foundation of all of your other goals. Your Soul Purpose statement is an anchor statement, similar to a vision statement, which clearly states the impact that you desire to make on the world. It is also a declaration that drives you because it is at the core of everything you do and everything you say. Trust me—this is the quickest and fastest way to make sure that your Values are going to line up with your goals to create ease for the Law of Attraction to work in your life. Over the past ten years, I have tweaked my Soul Purpose statement a bit, as my experience has helped me hone in on my core purpose and offerings to the world. And you will too. There will be words that resonate with you at one time and not at another. Pay attention and simply make those tweaks.

MY SOUL PURPOSE

My Soul Purpose is to help others make lots (and lots) of money so they can expand their impact, give back to the organizations they care about, AND live a great life.

YOUR SOUL PURPOSE

_____

_____

_____

_____

WRITE ALL OF YOUR GOALS DOWN

Next, begin to write, without judgment, fifty goals that you would like to accomplish in the next twelve months. To add power to them, state them in the present tense as if you are already accomplishing them. Brian Tracy's book on goals originally led me to the idea of writing down at least fifty goals. For some reason, there is magic in writing fifty goals. It will stretch you and then you will begin to get to the core of what it is you really want. One of my Synchronize clients went through this process, and she said it was so powerful because she easily got to fifty, but then she was just "done." There wasn't another goal left.

Also, be specific! This is YOUR LIFE! Again, it is very important that you just "free write" without any internal dialogue or criticism. As humans, it is easy for us to want to criticize what we are saying or putting out there, but this exercise is to be done without judgment. Be as specific as possible. Take at least fifteen minutes, if not more. Just keep writing until you can no longer write anymore.

Also, make sure that they are quantifiable goals—that they have a beginning and an end—rather than goals of "being" (i.e. more confident, a better spouse, etc.). You may be able to quantify "being" goals in some way. For instance, notice that one of my goals is to "commit time every day to grow spiritually" rather than "be more spiritual." The goal I wrote down is quantifiable action, not a goal of "being."

_____

_____

_____

_____

_____

_____

_____

_____

_____

_____

_____

_____

_____

Narrow Your Fifty Goals to Your Top Ten

My Examples:

Give back to organizations by acting in a leadership role

Write books that inspire, motivate, and change lives

Write a New York Times Bestseller

Be a highly-paid and sought-after speaker who inspires, motivates, and changes lives

Live on the coast with a view of the ocean

Take a week off every month to recharge/Design an amazing ideal schedule

Develop a web presence that inspires, motivates, and changes lives by helping people stay on track

Deliver training that inspires, motivates, and changes lives

Give freely to my favorite non-profits every month

Write and publish a novel (for fun!)

Your List of Goals:

_____

_____

_____

_____

_____

_____

_____

_____

_____

_____

Now, look back at your list. Again, this is without judgment. Just notice what is there. Notice what you have written down. Does anything surprise you? Does anything stand out for you? Do you notice any themes or patterns?

_____

_____

_____

_____

_____

_____

_____

_____

_____

_____

_____

As I looked at my list, I realized that there were some themes going on. Overall, I wanted to change lives and help others live in their greatest potential, which tied back to my Soul Purpose. I also noticed that I wanted to be living in my own unlimited potential. That all made sense since the name of my corporation is, and always has been, Potential Quest, Inc.! By helping others achieve their greatest potential, I would also move toward my own potential. Wow!

Identify Your Top 5

Look back at your list again. First, cross out the five goals that you are willing to release. This might be difficult because it is forcing you to choose, but looking at the list, ask yourself, *"If I had to let go of five of these goals so that I could discover my One Great Goal, which would they be?"* Do not spend time going over and over the list. Just pick the five that jump out at you and cross them off. It doesn't mean that you won't achieve them, but it does mean that you might have to let go for a moment to discover what you really want.

My List of Goals:

1. Give back to organizations by acting in a leadership role
2. Write books that inspire, motivate, and change lives
3. Write a New York Times Bestseller
4. Be a highly-paid and sought-after speaker who inspires, motivates, and changes lives
5. ~~Live on the coast with a view of the ocean~~
6. ~~Take a week off every month to recharge/Design an amazing ideal schedule~~
7. ~~Develop a web presence that inspires, motivates, and changes lives by helping people stay on track~~
8. Deliver training that inspires, motivates, and changes lives
9. Give freely to my favorite non-profits every month
10. ~~Write and publish a novel (for fun!)~~

Choose Your Top 2

There are five goals left. Your top five goals. Once you have the top five left, then eliminate three more (leaving two), framing it this way, *"If I could only achieve these top two goals in my lifetime, what would they be?"*

My List of Goals:

1. ~~Give back to organizations by acting in a leadership role~~
2. Write books that inspire, motivate, and change lives
3. ~~Write a New York Times Bestseller~~
4. Be a highly-paid and sought-after speaker who inspires, motivates, and changes lives
5. ~~Live on the coast with a view of the ocean~~
6. ~~Take a week off every month to recharge/Design an amazing ideal schedule~~
7. ~~Develop a web presence that inspires, motivates, and changes lives by helping people stay on track~~
8. ~~Deliver training that inspires, motivates, and changes lives~~
9. ~~Give freely to my favorite non-profits every month~~
10. ~~Write and publish a novel (for fun!)~~

Your One Great Goal

Once you have eliminated three more and chosen the final two, you then need to ask yourself, *"If I could achieve just one of these two goals in my lifetime, what would it be?"* Then **<u>underline</u>** that goal. I've taken thousands of people through this process and one thing I know is that some people easily get to, and identify, their One Great Goal and others end up with two goals at the top of their list that are very similar. If that happened for you, simply combine the two goals and make them one—that is your One Great Goal.

My List of Goals:

1. ~~Give back to organizations by acting in a leadership role~~

2. Write books that inspire, motivate, and change lives

3. ~~Write a New York Times Bestseller~~

4. **<u>Be a highly-paid</u> <u>and sought-after speaker who inspires, motivates, and changes lives</u>**

5. ~~Live on the coast with a view of the ocean~~

6. ~~Take a week off every month to recharge/Design an amazing ideal schedule~~

7. ~~Develop a web presence that inspires, motivates, and changes lives by helping people stay on track~~

8. ~~Deliver training that inspires, motivates, and changes lives~~

9. ~~Give freely to my favorite non-profits every month~~

10. ~~Write and publish a novel (for fun!)~~

Congratulations! You have chosen your One Great Goal!

A Triple Check

Are you surprised at the goals on your list? Knowing your One Great Goal is the first step to clarity. The truth is, the rest of your goals will come true as well and I will show you the best way to write them down to allow them to easily come into creation for you.

Before you continue on, though, take a moment and double check whether or not you are in alignment with every single goal on your list. Start with #1 and work your way backwards.

I have found that the easiest way to determine whether or not your goals are in alignment with YOU (the real you, your higher self, etc.) is to do a Triple Check. A Triple Check simply means that you check to see if each goal is in alignment with your Mind, Body, and Spirit. If a goal isn't in alignment with one of the three, it probably will be very difficult to create. If it is in alignment with all three areas of you, WOOOHOOOO, you are on your way!

There is nothing I love more than seeing my clients' dreams form into reality. The interesting thing is that most of my clients decide to work with me because they want to reach their sales goals. Then they quickly realize that there's so much more to our sales training and coaching programs than they ever imagined.

My clients know there is something missing regarding why they aren't reaching their goals, but they aren't sure what it is. They don't know why they keep getting stuck or reaching the same sales results every month. There are often key things that are missing from how they are moving from their sales goals to their dream goals. I find, as humans, we often start from exactly where we are. We set mediocre sales goals that get us "just enough" and then wonder why we aren't getting anywhere.

But that's backward. You have to start with the end in mind.

YOUR SALES AND INCOME GOAL

I imagine that your sales or income goal ended up somewhere on your list of ten goals. It doesn't really matter where it ended up (first or last), it just needs to be somewhere on there. If it's not on the list at all, I'd be wondering if you still want to be in business or want to continue on as a sales professional. But for most of you, it was on the list.

How you choose your sales or income goal is really important because you need to have a sales goal that is in alignment with you if you are going to reach it. If you have performed the Triple Check and the goal doesn't feel quite right and is out of alignment in an area, then I want you to implement this exercise to help you find the best number for you.

First, choose a range. What are the highest and the lowest ranges for your sales goal that you can imagine? If you can imagine it, play with doubling your sales.

Highest: _____

Lowest: _____

Next, choose a number (between the highest and the lowest) that feels the best to you.

Number Between that Feels Good: _____

Then, do the Triple Check again. Is it in alignment now? Bingo! That's your number!

Take a moment and write this narrative as if it's 90 days in the future and you've achieved all of these things:

_____

_____

_____

_____

_____

_____

_____

Your sales plan must be connected to your dreams for it all to work together. For a lot of people, there's a major disconnect with this. They create the dream life and goals, but they never connect it back to their sales plan. The key here is to determine how much money you need to make to live your dream life. Now, remember, I am assuming in all of this that you are serving your clients at the highest level and that you are only working with clients whose problems you can solve. In other words, this entire plan only works if you are coming from a place of complete integrity.

Assuming this is true, then break down the exact number of sales you need every month to live your dream life. For example, if your annual sales goal is $250,000, then your monthly sales goal would be $20,833.

Break it down one more step by determining how many clients (on average) it will take each month and how many appointments you need. For example, if you average $3,000 per client, then you'll need to sign 7 clients every month. To know how many appointments you need to land your 7 clients, look at your closing ratio. If your closing ratio is 50%, then you'll need at least 14 appointments with potential clients to reach your goal.

Number of Clients:

_____

Number of Appointments:

_____

Once you know these, you can determine how many sales calls you need to make to reach your appointment goal. If you know that you schedule 50% of the time when you're making sales calls, then you'll need to make at least 28 qualified sales appointments that month.

Number of Sales Calls: _____

Yes, it's painful to break it down to that granular of a level. But once you know that information, you have freedom and are on your way to reaching your dreams!

For those of you who want to fast-track this process and double your sales even faster, I want to flip a belief on its head for you. You no longer have 30 days in a month. Instead, you have 15 days. I refer to this process as "The Power of 15," so it's easy to remember! If you need 28 qualified appointments to reach your goal (again, these are averages), schedule those 28 appointments in the first 15 days of the month. I can almost guarantee that if you do that, you will reach your goal. I was once brought into a company to help a sales professional reach his goal because his company was going to fire him. The stakes were extremely high. He'd been averaging approximately $12,000 per month and needed to sell $50,000 the next month just to keep his job. I explained this process to him. He launched his month with an extreme sense of urgency to reach his goal of 20 appointments in the first 15 days. Now, some of his appointments happened later in the month, but guess what? He reached his goal that month. I saw him at the very end of the month at one of my sales conferences and he was so happy! He came running over and said, "Guess what?!? I reached my sales goal of $50,000! And, I quit my job and found a better one!"

CLARITY CHANGES EVERYTHING

According to Brian Tracy, the Law of Clarity matters most, "Clarity accounts for probably 80% of success and Lack of clarity is probably more responsible for frustration and underachievement than any other single factor. That's why we say that 'Success is goals, and all else is commentary.'"

The only way to reach the sales and income goals you've been thinking about is to create the dream life and the goals you REALLY want. These are the dreams you think about right before you go to bed—the dreams you think about right when you wake up. They are those thoughts and dreams you push down because you don't think they are possible. You believe they are so far outside of what you've ever accomplished in the past.

When you do this—when you allow yourself to discover the dreams that have become dormant—then you finally begin to head in the right direction.

In 2012, as I was finishing up *Selling With Synchronicity*, I felt the need to simplify...again. In a decade of growing my business, I'd launched and tweaked and ended a lot of programs, most of which were huge successes. It's just that I am always looking for the quickest and fastest way to get people the results they need, so when the inspiration to simplify came again, I listened and sought the clarity I needed.

Through the clarifying process that I use with my own clients, I was able to identify the simplest and most powerful business model I'd ever imagined. I decided to keep my Sales Camps and my Synchronize programs going, and to keep speaking to fill those programs; but I let go of everything else—the smaller programs I had been offering, the huge LIVE event I'd been putting on for years, and so many other things that had begun to clutter my schedule, my business, and my life.

It was a little scary to think about chopping off so many branches at once, but the idea of it also felt like a huge relief. I was clear that I needed more simplicity. I needed fewer steps to get the same (and actually better) results. I needed more space and downtime in my life.

What occurred in my business after that was nothing short of miraculous! How could one possibly make more money with less programs and offerings? Well, I was about to find out!

And now, you've got clarity as well. You've got the dream life plan. You've created your sales plan and it's connected to your dream life. Beautiful! Feeling free yet? Okay, there's one more step. Well, wait, there are many more steps because you have to get moving! You will find, though, that by having this clear plan, the inspired ideas to move forward begin to show up. But then, it's up to you. You have to take that first step in front of you, which will be out of your Comfort Zone. I'm telling you, you probably won't want to do it, but it's the exact step you have to take. Are you ready?

QUANTUM CORNER

BECCAH LEINDECKER
Keller Williams Realty
www.timelessvaluehomes.com

SINCE SALES CAMP and Synchronize coaching with Rebekah and Ursula, I have gone from generating little to no sales on my own to running my own business and generating $5 million in business in a little over a year.

When I attended Sales Camp, I needed clarity on The How and The Who. Who was I going to target? How was I going to do it? And of course, can I do it?

My One Great Goal came down to a dollar amount of money I wanted to make because that amount would allow me to live the life I desired. I had several goals, and they will all come true when I make that amount. Initially, I didn't like that my one great goal was about money. Ursula helped me to reframe my thinking around the goal of making more money, and now that number motivates me.

Any success I have comes to me when I am feeling in love with my life and trusting that I will reach my goals. I work towards my goals, take the actions necessary, and then trust that my goals will come to fruition. I give gratitude for my day and my opportunities, even if things are not going exactly as I would like. Even when I was in Synchronize, I went through some hard times! I went months without sales or hopes of a sale, and at one time, I even started thinking about getting another job. Thankfully, I trusted that good things would happen to me in my life and my career because I have so much passion for what I do. After going through that experience of feeling totally defeated and seeing what happened on the other side, I am able to stay calm and trust the universe will work everything out.

At Sales Camp, I came in with a Limiting Belief that sales people were viewed as not genuine. I knew I was a sales person, and I knew that I was genuine, but I still thought people might view me as less than genuine due to my occupation.

I also had an image of a life I wanted and I knew it could be possible. However, I started out my career in real estate with a team that guilted me for not being in the office all of the time, and told stories of how they worked their lives away and that is why they were successful. I could appreciate that, but I knew I did not want that life. My goal was to live a life of balance, travel, and service. I set the goal of working 20 hours or less a week, and still completely servicing my clients while hitting my income goals. With my background, I felt bad for even making that a goal. I knew people would laugh or even think poorly of me.

I set the new belief that people love working with me, and I work 20 hours or less each week and continue to hit my goals. When you find a belief that really resonates with you, and let go of the old beliefs, it feels freeing. It feels like you don't have to pretend to think this or that it's bad. When I truly started to believe this, my entire life transformed.

My new beliefs are the number one reason for my success!

Do you know how much energy it takes to fight off Limiting Beliefs, instead of finding a belief that rings true with you? I was able to accomplish so much more. I found out what activities were bringing in my business by tracking my numbers, and focused on those activities. Every other activity, I found a way to delegate it. Most importantly, I believed and trusted that I could achieve my goals and ideal lifestyle. I started living my ideal lifestyle, even when I wasn't sure if I should, or if I had enough money, or if I would have enough clients coming in. I trusted. And, I focused on targeting clients that I enjoyed working with, and not taking on clients that would make me feel miserable in my job. It's amazing how much you can love your job and your life when you work with people you enjoy!

In the year that I finally made those shifts, I did work an average of 20 hours or less each week, traveled/vacationed 13 times, and closed $1 million dollars in volume in one month. I went from working all the time and never getting my own clients, to living a lovely balanced life and closing all of my own clients!

Sales is amazing because you are the expert, and when you are working with your clients' best interest at heart, you are serving and advising people in their big decisions. Our role as sales people is SO important.

I am beyond excited about my future. I am so grateful to everything that has transpired so far, and I know that I am moving in the direction of my dreams. Focus on what you want and you will see that appear in your life. Just the other day, I was reminded of this again. I have always had a passion for historic homes, so I preview every single home that comes on the market in a particular historic homes neighborhood. On a Monday, I previewed the homes just as I always do. On Tuesday morning, I received a call giving me a lead that's searching for a million-dollar home in the exact neighborhood I previewed the day before. Now this is what happens in a New Belief Zone!

STEP #2: WRITE

"Goals in writing are dreams with deadlines."

~ Brian Tracy ~

Sitting at my desk, setting my intention the way I did every day, I wrote it again in my journal: *Move back to Minnesota.* I dropped my pen when I was done and shook my head, wondering how long I would write this down before my husband and I would gather the courage to actually do it.

I looked at the other goals on the page: *Make Sales Coach Now a national brand. Double last year's revenue.*

How am I going to move back to Minnesota and achieve a national brand and double last year's income? I'd pretty much be starting over, in a new place, with new people. I'd have to spend time establishing my credibility there. And I don't even know if my people are there. Is there even a market for Sales Coach Now in Minnesota?

I wondered to myself if these two goals were so conflicted that I wasn't going to be able to achieve them both, but I noted how deep my desire was for both of them. I could feel the longing to live in Minnesota deep in my bones, and my desire to change lives with Sales Coach Now was just as deep and powerful.

I don't know how long it will take, I thought to myself in the quiet of the morning, *but I know that writing my goals on paper has been a powerful tool in achieving all of my goals. The promotions in the IT company... the business... the books I've written... the events I've created... the awards I've won... all of them were written in my journal for some time before they manifested.*

Letting my mind drift back through all of my achievements, I settled back into my chair and looked at the words written on the page: *Move back to Minnesota.*

Yes, I know it's going to happen. But right now, I just don't know how.

Journals Full of Checkboxes

For years, I wrote *Move back to Minnesota* in countless journals. I also asked all of my intuitive friends and anyone I deemed psychic if they saw us moving back to Minnesota because we just couldn't pull the trigger and were looking outside for validation or a sign that it was the right thing to do.

One of my dearest friends, who is also amazingly intuitive, told me multiple times that she saw us moving back but would edit her comments with, "but not right now." I saw her about a year before we moved back and she said, "I see it happening sooner than you might think, so be ready to do it." Even though I wanted to believe she was right, I blew it off.

But I kept writing it down in my journal, over and over and over again, *Move back to Minnesota. Move back to Minnesota.*

Move back to Minnesota. Every time I wrote it down, I put a little checkbox right in front of it. Little did I know how powerful that small act was.

Every significant goal that I have achieved, I have written down first at some point. From writing my books, to receiving awards and yes, even: *Have a baby.* ALL of those items have been on my list and in my journal at some point.

Writing *Move back to Minnesota* was just a natural part of my goal-setting process that was going to open up that path.

Bringing It Into the Physical

Did you know that 99% of goals happen just by writing them down? Yes, sadly, 85% of the population (maybe even less) will never write their goals down. We underestimate the power of writing our goals down because we think it's not enough, and I think it's because we don't make the Quantum Physics connection.

What is the act of writing down a goal, really? Isn't it the act of bringing something out of thought and imagination and making it a physical reality with ink and paper? Up until the moment you write it, it's just a thought...an idea? Of course, those are pretty powerful on their own, but what happens when you use your own physical energy to put that thought or idea on physical paper? Aren't you making it a physical reality in some way...and adding your own energy of intention to that idea or thought?

Never underestimate the power of writing something down, particularly the goals you are planning to create.

I'm a huge advocate for *handwriting* your goals in a special journal instead of typing them up. The reason is because something magical happens between your fingers and your brain as you are writing. The action with your fingers directly wires it into your subconscious, and your subconscious begins to work on it immediately. And remember, your subconscious is wired directly to the super conscious, which is why the Universe begins to conspire on your behalf.

Checkbox Technology

As I was reviewing my own goals, I noticed that my process of goal creation had changed over the years. It had evolved. Two of the main changes were *how* and *where* I was writing them down. This process evolved slowly over time, but I have no doubt that this new way of writing my goals down was paramount in easily achieving them!

When I was in the corporate world, a good friend of mine wrote her goals for the day down on a legal notepad every single day. She put little checkboxes on the notepad and then checked off her "to do's" as she went through her day. I noticed that she got more done during the day and also always reached her sales stretch goal each month.

Struggling to reach my sales goals at the time, I was willing to try anything and figured I better implement that habit as well. And it was amazing what began to happen—I started to reach my goals much more quickly and easily.

(It wasn't until later I learned that statistics tell us our productivity goes up 25% simply by writing our goals down and 90% of our goals get completed when you write them down, even if you never look at the list again! Did you get that? 90% percent of your goals get completed simply by writing them down, even if you forget about them. The tragedy is that most people never even take the time to write their goals down because their belief system doesn't allow them to do that one simple, powerful act.)

As I went along each day, I happily checked off the tasks on my list. Even better, I started to reach my daily sales goals, which ultimately helped me reach my monthly sales goals.

But it gets even better.

In the beginning, I would write about my goals in a small journal. It was my "dreamer" journal and I would write about all of the things that I wanted to create with words like: *I want to... I will create...* While it was helpful, I didn't feel like it was a clear request to the Universe.

Over time, without thinking much about it, I started to use this same "checkbox" methodology for my goal list, putting put a box in front of each goal that I wrote down. And I wrote it the same way I wrote my task list, *in the present tense, expecting that it would get done easily and effortlessly.*

 Thank about how important this is! I didn't get it at the time, but as I look back at all of the goals I have accomplished, a big part of the work was writing the goals down on my Expected Goal List! As I was working on this book, I found my goal list from 2012. I had written 50 goals down as part of an assignment from one of my coaches at the time. I'm going to share that goal list with you here so you can see how powerful it really was—and is—to write goals down and get into a New Belief Zone that will get us there. Although not every goal on this list was achieved, the goals that were most in alignment with me at the time DID come true. What was really interesting is that back then I didn't write them in the present tense, because I didn't realize that would help, and yet it still worked. What I know now, though, is that when I write them in the present tense, *they happen faster*!

- Attract a traditional publisher
- $25,000 in sponsorship dollars
- $150,000 in after event sales (specific event)
- $30K at LE Event
- Sell Ocean Shores
- Become Debt Free
- Travel to Italy
- Travel to Hawaii
- Take a Mediterranean Cruise with family
- Move to Minnesota
- Purchase a cute house
- Find a new amazing spa to write
- Publish my novel
- Finish writing Selling With Synchronicity
- Speak on other people's stages
- Become pregnant
- Purchase a special wardrobe for work
- Purchase the new make-up
- Make more than $25,000 per month
- Do more events with industry leaders
- Speak at industry known author event (2X)
- Work weekly at the spa
- Receive regular massages
- Create meaningful new programs for clients
- Create a virtual business

- Grow retirement account to $50K+
- Get life insurance
- Speak nationally
- Get paid to speak regularly
- Work out 4-5X/week
- Get in the best shape of my life
- Go with the flow
- Take all Fridays off
- Take the week at the end of the month off
- Speak in Italy
- Share the stage with Brian Tracy
- Be mentioned by Brian Tracy
- Fly 1st class
- Have $50K+ in the bank
- Purchase more rental properties
- Pay rentals off
- Pay Student loans off
- Invest in Ti's certs
- Have better relationships with my sister/bros
- Create a vision board

Have a deep healing session

99% of these goals came true and a few of them are still in the works. I will leave the guessing up to your imagination. However, the main reason I am sharing this list with you is to motivate you to write those goals down! This is the Universe calling out to you to set the book down and take yourself through the exercise. Now. In this moment!

QUANTUM CORNER

BARBRA PORTZLINE, PHD

Organizational Rebel® LLC

www.organizationalrebel.com

SINCE SALES CAMP, I started a new business that has multiple revenue streams, and is targeted to replace my full-time income within 6 months and double it (at a minimum) within the first year. My biggest issue was that I didn't know how to clearly communicate the value of what I do—and now I do! That clarity gave me the momentum to move forward. My biggest discovery was that I realized how I kept telling myself a very self-deprecating story about my value regardless of how "together" I appeared on the outside.

The new habits that helped me sync up was regularly stating affirmations, writing my vision and goals down, and not worrying about things that are out of my control. Before Sales Camp, I believed that selling = being inauthentic, and I believed that I would screw things up again the way I did before. At Sales Camp, my new belief became, "I am a highly skilled business strategist. I inspire, empower, and educate people on how to live their dreams and build a profitable business aligned with their vision." This has been an empowering and freeing experience because it helped me own my worth and step into my power. The actions that helped me the most include ongoing coaching and accountability, writing out my projections, and tracking my success. NOW I know that selling is ridiculously easy! I now know that I truly believe I can live the life I want. I believe that I can thrive, not only survive. I believe that with intention and action, we can make magic!

CHANGING THE HOW

Your Expected Goal Checklist is the list of fifty goals that you created during the One Great Goal process and your top ten goals written down on a legal pad with a checkbox in front of each one because you actually expect it to happen. This is where the power of expectation comes in!

Think about it. If you expected something to happen, how would you write it down? Go back and look at your list of ten goals. Now, if you need to, rewrite each one in *present tense*, as if you expect it to happen. Notice the words that you choose. Then remember to put the checkbox in front of each one.

I am a best-selling author.

I live in Hawaii and have an amazing and joy filled life.

My business revenues exceed $1M.

My body is in full and complete health.

My sales have tripled.

I am sharing this journey with the love of my life.

I travel first class wherever I go.

I eat only organic and fresh foods daily.

I am serving my top 20% of clients on a daily basis.

I am an award-winning speaker.

Also, a note regarding how many goals to write down on your extended goal list. Remember to begin with 50 and then prioritize down to 10 before you go through the One Great Goal process. Either focus on those 10 or you may decide to focus on 5 to start with now and leave the other 5 for later. Some people decide to only focus on their One Great Goal for now because they trust that the rest of the goals on their list will be coming anyway (that's their belief). Go with whatever feels most in alignment with you. Triple Check it if you need to.

Review the list daily if you can. Reviewing regularly isn't because you doubt that it will happen. Instead, use the daily 5-minute review to imagine that the goals have all come to fruition. Spend at least one minute with each goal and get into the feeling of what it will be like when you achieve that goal. The feeling is really important. The great feeling you experience when you think about it is the feeling of creation. THAT feeling is what will allow your goals to show up even faster. If you feel any feelings of doubt coming up, let those feelings go and focus again on what you are creating.

CHANGING THE WHERE

Your goal list should be on your legal pad. Then, I want you to grab a brand new journal to keep track of the evidence you see showing up for you. Write your goals on the first page of the journal with checkboxes and then only use this journal to write down the evidence that shows you that your goals are coming to fruition.

For example, one of my goals was to win awards for my books. I would have been happy with one award, but I decided not to limit myself on the amount of awards I could win. In fact, I had written on my goal list, "Win multiple awards for my books." Asking big is in my blood, and should be in yours, too!

Once I set that goal, I got excited whenever I received an email from the awards organization giving an update on the contest. Every time I got that email, I believed it was evidence that I was going to receive an email soon that confirmed I had won an award and perhaps multiple awards. I got excited about that! And every time an email came in, my feeling of winning and my belief that it was going to happen got stronger. And then the emails started flying in telling me that I had won five awards for three of my books!

Keeping track of the evidence that your goal is coming to fruition will keep you motivated and on track.

EXTRA CREDIT: DON'T BE SHY

One you've written the goals, then tell someone, but only tell someone you trust. Saying it out loud is even more powerful than writing it because it's like you are putting your order in to the Universe. The Universe already heard you when you wrote it down, but saying it out loud is like supercharging it.

In all my Sales Camp courses and LIVE Synchronize coaching events, I am always taking my clients through this process of writing and then verbalizing their goals. It's like putting their goal on a high-speed train!

Then, it's important to future pace it.

Imagine that the goal has already occurred in the future and be in a moment of celebration.

Then, see a timeline in your mind of how you got there from the moment you first did the visualization. What's amazing is that the first one or two steps are already there—you will be able to see them!

Finally, put your right hand on your heart before you open your eyes and just think about it feels like to achieve that goal. By putting your hand on your heart, you are anchoring that feeling in. Remember to come back to that feeling anytime you need to be reenergized to reach your goal.

SUPERCHARGE WITH SCRIPTING

If you are ready to super-charge your goals, then consider scripting. It's a technique that I've noticed has become really popular in recent years. The best way I've ever seen scripting done, and the technique we use with our clients during Sales Camp, is to choose a new, separate journal, find a blank page, and write a future date at the top of that page—the date by which you would love your goals to come to fruition. Then, write a journal entry as if all of the goals on your list have come to fruition. You might start it out with something like, "It's December 31st, 2017, and I've just had the most incredible year I could imagine! It began by hosting a very powerful and profitable Quantum Sales Summit, followed by the launch of my podcast, and the release of my fourth non-fiction book with a notable publisher. We doubled the sales of the company again while working only 20 hours per week. I was so glad to spend so much quality time with Tim and Lucca as we traveled to Italy, Napa, and St. Thomas. Our remodel is finished, the pontoon rides with friends this summer were amazing, and Lucca can now swim like a dolphin!"

Feel free to add more or less. Just make sure that it makes your heart sing and resonates with you on every level. Remember, this is your opportunity to script out the perfect outcome.

ANGIE WEBER

tena.cious edge

www.tenaciousedge.com

B EFORE SALES CAMP, my biggest Limiting Belief (*which kept me in my Comfort Zone*) was that I was bugging people when following up with them, resulting in lost leads and little coming in from sales since I would give up after 1 or 2 touches.

When I stretched my Belief Zone and changed my belief to knowing people *wanted* to hear from me, I immediately saw results in my sales, confidence, and how I showed up to networking events.

In fact, by using a tracking sheet, I have been able to quadruple my monthly sales and often get thanked for following up with people who tell me I'm very "tenacious."

After the first Sales Camp and following along as Tena Pettis went through Synchronize, we doubled our sales for tena.cious. The second time I went to Sales Camp, I doubled my personal sales goal 5 days before the end of the shortest month of the year! And that got me my beautiful gold watch!

I really needed to learn how to be a "sales person." There were a lot of Limiting Beliefs around being too pushy and the internal fear that I could *never* sell "that" much. I needed help getting rid of those beliefs, but also the tools to use when selling to help me feel more confident.

Looking back at the last two times that I have attended Sales Camp, I always chuckle a little because the goals I had written down were pretty small compared to where I am now. I realized the more I wrote them down, the less intimidating they seemed to be. It was a lot easier to get to my goals than I thought. The #1 habit that I created was to follow up. It's the number one thing that I have learned will get me to my goal, but also having the abundance mindset of allowing sales to come to me.

Before Sales Camp, I did not want to be that sleazy-used-cars-salesperson kind of person that everyone runs and hides from. I thought of sales as pushy, hard, and honestly a little yucky. I also believed that my goals were way too far out of reach. There was no way little ol' me could do these goals I had written down.

Since Sales Camp, I know that I'm not being pushy. I'm being *persistent* and people respect that. There are people out there that want and need what I have to offer, and I am the one doing a disservice to them if I am not following up or offering them what we've got. When I finally realized that those goals are totally doable, it felt like I was getting lifted out of a fog and all of this new opportunity was in front of me. And new opportunity stirs up a lot of excitement!

Being in a New Belief Zone gave me the confidence that I needed to keep going after the goals. Even if I hear NO, I move on to the next one! The main actions that helped me the most were that I started building up my pipeline, I opened up my work in progress sheet every morning so I knew who I had to follow up with, and I set my intentions and visualized what

I wanted—I could feel that gold watch on my wrist! Now I KNOW that selling can be fun and easy! And, it gets better! Since Sales Camp, I have launched another business and it has given me the confidence in both businesses to go after some really crazy goals, although I know I will look back at them next time and realize they weren't that scary!

Step #3: Sync

*"You can live your life angry, bitter, mad at somebody or even guilty,
not letting go of your own mistakes,
but you won't receive the good things God has in store for you."*

~ Joel Osteen ~

"I DON'T KNOW. Maybe we'll just adopt. We're open to having a baby no matter how it comes," I said, knowing that wasn't the truth but trying to convince myself more than her. It seemed like all of my friends and colleagues were pregnant at the same time and I could feel them look at me with sad eyes when they didn't think I was looking. The truth was, I wasn't ready to give up on my dream—our dream—to have a baby naturally.

"Urs, I can't wait 'til you have your baby. I know this is going to happen for you. I believe..." she started, and then lit up with excitement as the idea hit her: "What if this isn't any different than all of the other goals you've achieved?"

The energy of what she said hit me full force, but I couldn't wrap my head around it. "What do you mean?"

"Well, what if you used all of the same skills and tools you have used to double and triple your sales and help others do the same...on this dream of having a baby...and moving back to Minnesota?"

I sat back in the spa—that's where we do all of our best brainstorming about life and business—and let it sink in.

Yeah, what if I did?

She let me sit with it for a while and then turned the tables on me, asking me the questions that I should have been asking myself, "You're clear that you want a baby and that you want to raise that baby in Minnesota with your family. I'm certain you've been writing it down. And now, you just need to do the rest of what you do with your goals, right? What's the next step in your process? What is keeping this baby from coming to you...and keeping you from just getting up and moving to Minnesota?"

As soon as she asked the questions, I noticed the tension in my body and the inner conflict that was coming up for me again around having a baby and moving back to my home state. And then I searched for the next step in my process and how to integrate it here...and I laughed out loud.

I need to let go. All of this tension and inner conflict isn't the frequency that will attract what I want. I need to let go of the How and When. And just step into the vibration that is a match for what I want.

STOP SQUEEZING

One of the reasons we didn't move back to Minnesota for a long time is because I squeezed the life out of that goal! I stalked it. I haunted it. I scared it when it wasn't looking. Get the picture?

I was holding on so tight that even if that goal wanted to spring to life, it couldn't breathe!

I talked about moving back so much to my close circle that it was the first thing they would ask me when they saw me, "So, have you made a decision yet?"

"No, nope, definitely not yet but I've redone my pro con list at least one hundred times by now!" I'd answer.

After a few years, that got pretty old. From everything that I had read, I knew it wasn't a good idea to stalk a goal. It was a terrible idea. What became really clear to me is that when I focused on a goal too much, what I was really saying to the Universe, or what my "frequency" was saying was, "I don't have that goal. I don't have that goal."

I was focusing on the wrong thing.

The same thing was true when it came to having a baby. Instead of continuing to believe I was infertile, I took a leap of faith and opened up the belief that it just might be possible to get pregnant at almost 39 years old. I stopped Googling all of the articles that told me I only had a 5% chance of getting pregnant. I stopped listening to people who told me that my eggs had almost all dried up and raised my frequency in this area, allowing me to move into a New Belief Zone.

I released all that old B.S., and I started to feel hopeful. Eventually hope led to joy and even expectation.

Two months before I got pregnant, I was told by a friend of mine (who is super intuitive) that not only would I get pregnant, I would have a boy. And he was on his way.

Two months later, I was pregnant. Four months after she told me, I found out I was pregnant with a boy.

FREQUENCY AND THE LAW OF REVERSED EFFORT

We've already talked about the Law of Attraction, and that law and so many others words on the principle of Frequency. You see, all thoughts, feelings, beliefs, and even words have a frequency. The powerful thoughts, feelings, beliefs, and words vibrate at a high frequency in your New Belief Zone; and the disempowering thoughts, feelings, beliefs, and words vibrate at a lower, heavier frequency in the old energy shield of your Comfort Zone.

Dr. Masaru Emoto's (Japanese author and researcher) groundbreaking work showed us how our thoughts and feelings impact the structure of water when frozen. His experiments demonstrated that negative words like "hate" changed the molecular structure of the water when frozen, making it look murky and gross, whereas words like "love" and "gratitude" made crystals that were structurally more symmetrical, healthy-looking, and beautiful to observe. Since our bodies are mostly made of water, he suggested that our negative thoughts cause much of the dis-ease we experience in our bodies. While his claims have been disputed by many scientists, he has followers and believers all over the world because of his belief that, "Water is the mirror that has the ability to show us what we cannot see. It is the blueprint for our reality, which can change with a single, positive thought. All it takes is faith, if you're open to it."

So, if we are thinking, feeling, believing, speaking, and operating at a low frequency while our goals and dreams are vibrating at a high frequency, we will never be able to achieve them until we expand into a new energy field, which is our New Belief Zone.

You might not want to hear this, but here goes. It difficult to receive what you want if you feel negative al time and if you spread negativity to others. Yes, we will all have bad days, but if you spend more of your time in a frequency of negativity, you are going to have a lot of negative things happening in your life.

In my case, I was living in the frequency of Infertility until I synced up with the frequency of Pregnancy by changing my thoughts, feelings, words, and actions when it came to talking baby.

So syncing is really the step of stepping into the same frequency that what you want is vibrating at. You want to become a match for what you want, so that it can be attracted to you.

Writing your goals down and reviewing them once a day is a great habit to create to keep you on track. However, holding your goals too tightly can have the opposite effect and make it even more difficult for you to achieve your goals.

What?

Yes, you read that correctly. Remember the statistic from the earlier chapter? 90% of goals get completed simply by writing them down as long as they are in alignment with your belief system. As long as they are in alignment with your frequency.

So why does focusing TOO much on your goals stop them from coming into creation?

That's a great question and I am going to do my best to answer it. I would wager that most people, even scientists, cannot answer this question, but this is my best guess.

It's because when you focus too much on them and feel like you are pushing or stressing to make them happen, you actually have a hidden belief that says, "I don't actually think my goal is going to happen" and all you're doing is reinforcing the frequency of "I don't have this right now. I don't have this right now. I don't have this right now."

You can try too hard and not get anywhere. My husband loves to say, "Trying is failing with honor." The key, as we've already discussed, is to make a decision that you will succeed no matter what. When you move beyond trying and have made a clear decision to succeed, then you also have to let go a little bit.

What do I mean by that?

You need to detach from the end result. Do all of the work we've discussed to this point and then let go because that will allow your frequency to rise.

Aldous Huxley is given credit for talking about the *"Law of Reversed Effort,"* but many others have been talking about it for a long time. Huxley said, "The harder we try with the conscious will to do something, the less we shall succeed. Proficiency and the results of proficiency come only to those who have learned the paradoxical art of doing and not doing, or combining relaxation with activity, of letting go as a person in order that the immanent and transcendent Unknown Quantity may take hold. We cannot make ourselves understand; the most we can do is to foster a state of mind, in which understanding may come to us." In other words, "A watched pot doesn't boil." I find that this shows up especially when we *need* sales to come in or when we feel like we are forcing a goal to happen. Have you ever had that feeling? (I feel you nodding your head.) We've all had that feeling. There are times when we try to force something to get done, but it just doesn't seem to happen. Why? We are forcing it. When you understand that letting go of something allows it to show up faster, you might be more inclined to follow inspired action and play more.

Plus, notice his words. Huxley says, "Foster a state of mind in which understanding may come to us." This state of mind that he mentions is really a state of high frequency.

Shift your energy and move into a higher frequency.

GRATITUDE

When you are in a state and feeling of gratitude, you are going to get more good things showing up for you. And, a state of gratitude is much more than thinking positively. It's really about being grateful for this moment in time, even though things aren't exactly as you'd like them to be and you have massive desires springing out of your heart and brain all of the time. But before you can KNOW that your goal is coming for sure AND be ready to RECEIVE it, you have to get into sync with it!

Wallace D. Wattles in the *Science of Getting Rich* states, "The desire for increase is inherent in all nature; it is the fundamental impulse of the universe... Every living thing is under this necessity for continuous advancement; where increase of life ceases, dissolution and death set in at once." And then he goes on to talk about Gratitude: "The more gratefully we fix our minds on the Supreme when good things come to us, the more good things we will receive, and the more rapidly they will come; and the reason simply is that the mental attitude of gratitude draws the mind into closer touch with the source from which the blessings come...You cannot exercise much power without gratitude; for it is gratitude that keeps you connected with Power."

Your desire for more is innate. You cannot change that, you can only get into sync with what you really desire by being grateful for what you have and believing that you CAN have all of the goals that you have written on your goal list.

And if you sync up to the frequency of Gratitude, then what you want will come to meet you because you will be in your New Belief Zone.

A Play Plan

If I have learned anything, it's that taking time to play allows my goals to happen even faster. Playing is hard for a lot of goal focused folks, and I can relate. In the corporate world, I learned that you have to work hard to succeed at anything. But it's not true. The more I incorporate play into my life, the easier things get for me.

Here's the thing, playing raises your frequency! It doesn't mean that I don't take action, I do. In fact, I often take action that is way outside of my Comfort Zone. But I still set my calendar and life up so that I can play. My intention is not to have a lot on my calendar the last week of the month so I can do the things that I really enjoy. For example, years ago I made the decision to work and do business at the spa so that my work would always feel like luxurious play—and it does! In fact, the spa that I do business with in Minnesota just gave me two free massages plus a free night's stay at any of their luxury hotels simply because I do business there. Do you see how play transforms into even more play?

Now that I have a toddler, I get to play even more! I have ample time with Lucca which allows me to completely focus on him and not on the goals I am working on. It seems like since we had Lucca, goals have come into creation even faster. Again, the Law of Reverse Effort is at play.

What's your Play Plan? What do you wish you could do more of? I promise you that by creating a Play Plan, you will not only enjoy your life more, you will raise your frequency and also bring your goals into reality even faster.

RISE TO THE FREQUENCY'S OCCASION

I knew I was getting into sync with my goals when I was standing backstage, about ready to go out and keynote, right behind Les Brown. Yes, THAT Les Brown!

Being on stage with Les Brown had been a goal on my list—only because I respect him so much!

Yet apparently, I wasn't specific enough about that goal. I should have said, "Speak on the stage with Les Brown and speak before him!" Instead, I became the closing keynote FOLLOWING Les on stage.

It sounds like a cool thing until you remember that it's Les Brown and that the audience is going to follow him out of the room to his table to connect with him because there wasn't a scheduled break. Plus, I was competing with dinner and a bathroom break. Not ideal!

But in that moment, I knew I had to bring it—and I had to be in a high frequency and a belief that I deserved to be on that stage with Les Brown. The second after I was introduced, I literally ran onto the stage, and with all of the confidence I could bring forth, I said, "Wait! I promise you that if you stay, I will give you the steps you need to double or triple your sales next year."

And then I paused. A very, very pregnant pause. I held my breath. Audience members stared at me and I stared back. Many were half out of their seats heading for Les, dinner, or the restroom.

And then, magically, most of them sat down. And I am telling you—I brought it that night on that stage. I had to match and even exceed the frequency of what had just occurred on that stage, and when I did...oooooh boy—talk about a dynamite experience for the audience and ME!

Later that night, my speaker agent told me that an events producer talked to her after the event and said that out of all the speakers, he was most interested in booking me and Les for his next event.

It showed me again the power of syncing up the frequency of what we want.

So what frequency are you ready to sync to?

QUANTUM CORNER

AMANDA RILEY

Amanda Riley Wellness

www.blissfulbalancemn.com

THROUGH SALES CAMP and Synchronize, I was able to double my sales; and this year, I plan to double again. Triple is even a possibility with the programs I was able to add in after clearing out the things that were holding me back.

I've always been confident with making money, but what I was looking for at Sales Camp was to just be a better business owner. My business needs me hands-on all the time, and I needed to learn and implement tools that allow my business to run while I'm away.

My One Great Goal was bringing in another healing mechanism that would generate income without me needing to do work. I didn't have the means or belief I was ready to bring it in. Shortly after I finished Synchronize, I was able to bring it in!!! Practicing gratitude has never been an issue for me, but I did have a problem with working 80-90+ hours a week, with little sleep and even less fun. I now cut out early on Wednesdays to have a date day with my daughter as soon as she is done with school, and I get 7 hours of sleep a night!!!

In the past, I believed that I needed to work sun up to sun down to be successful and to make money. I believed I needed to be available to all people all the time. I also believed I was living a happy life, and that because I was not tied down to a 9-5 job, I was free. Clearly, these were Limiting Beliefs that did not serve me.

Once I began focusing on my top 20%, I found people that could train when I was available. The realization that I was not free really rocked my world. When I took control of my schedule, I then realized what being free meant. I took 5 mini-vacations last year (the ocean is my recharge), and I work when I want to and I get to be with my daughter when I want to! The new belief opened up a space for me to sleep and have fun. Killing myself to help others be healthier is crazy! I took on the absolute belief that my clients will follow my lead and that was being more genuine. How can I tell my clients to get sleep and have fun when those two things do not exist in my world? Not anymore though!

The three habits that I developed that served me the most included intentional scheduling, figuring out every penny in and out, and delegation.

After shifting my beliefs at Sales Camp, I now KNOW that people can't wait to hear from me and when they do, they can't wait to buy from me! In my New Belief Zone, I also KNOW that I am on my way to being a million dollar a year earner, all while helping people become the best version of themselves!

Step #4: Shift

*"Your level of belief in yourself will inevitably
manifest itself in whatever you do."*

~ Les Brown ~

L ESS THAN A YEAR after that conversation with my friend
in the hot tub, I was speaking to a room full of sales
professionals and entrepreneurs in Minnesota... and glowing
with the joy of being three months pregnant.

That's a powerful businesswoman. There was a woman sitting
at my table who oozed confidence and influence.

She's definitely someone I need to know. I wasn't sure why—I
just felt the pull.

She introduced herself to me as Tena Pettis, from tena.cious,
a Social Media and Branding company that she had founded...
and we chatted for a little bit about speaking engagements that
she was interested in landing.

When the event was over, and I'd connected with a bunch of wonderful sales professionals and entrepreneurs, Tena walked over to me.

"Ursula, as I shared with you, I've been doing pretty well but I know that I can do more. I want to sign up for your next Sales Camp and I want to bring Angie with me." Angie was on her team.

"Oh, okay great! You know that it's in Southern California, right?" I asked, surprised that she was ready to not only pay for her team member, but that she was willing to travel to attend.

"Oh yeah. I know," she smiled. "Where do I sign us up?"

As I watched her walk away from the table, a new thought floated through my mind: *I wonder how many business owners there are here in Minnesota? And how many of them need my help?*

I had no idea that I had not only just found my first Minnesota client—my ideal client—but someone who would become one of the most important strategic partners I've ever had.

PARALLEL UNIVERSES

Have you ever had this experience? Life is going along as usual. Not necessarily good or bad. Just usual. And then something happens. Someone asks you a question that sparks a lightning bolt inspiration. Someone shares some insight with you that cracks open possibilities you never imagined. Or someone crosses your path with a story that makes you believe that what you want is really possible.

Regardless of the inciting incident, the experience feels like being launched into an alternate universe. Some of the characters and situations are the same, but better, more full of magic and ease, more real and joyful than the other one you were living in before.

Now, I've read a lot of books about Quantum Physics and parallel universes, and I think there really is something there, even if it's far too complex for me to understand or put into words here.

What isn't too complex for me to share is that this has been my experience on multiple occasions. One day, I was in the universe of "don't know how to sell" and only five years later, I was running a $20 million company. One instant, I was struggling to find a way to launch my business, and the next instant, connections I'd never dreamed of came into my world and launched me into a whole new experience in business.

And I'm not the only one. I can't tell you how many times clients have shifted one belief and contacted me to tell me that they were suddenly living in a world of synchronicity and ease in sales and business.

And now, I want to help you land in a "parallel universe," a New Belief Zone, that makes you excited to wake up to serve your clients and double and triple your revenue with ease and flow.

CHANGE YOUR BELIEFS AND CHANGE EVERYTHING

Now that you are clear on what you really want, you're writing your goals down, you're syncing your frequency to the vibration of what you want, it's finally time to identify your Limiting Beliefs and see what's really been stopping you. I love this part! Why do I get so excited about changing Limiting Beliefs? Because I've watched the "light bulb moment" occur and the results quickly follow.

So, let's get to work!

What would you have to believe to have a 6 or 7-figure business or to create a net worth of more than $1 million? Did you just take a deep inhale? Was there a part of you that hasn't even given yourself permission to dare take on this belief?

Stop for a moment and really think about that. Notice what is coming up for you. What are some of your immediate thoughts about how hard you'd have to work or how much time it would take to achieve those goals. Just notice because THOSE thoughts are tied to the beliefs that have stopped you from getting there.

For a long time, I believed that I had to work really, really hard to make a lot of money. I mean *hard*! Growing up on the farm, we worked physically hard, 24-7, so we could keep the farm running. I didn't really know anything else, but the belief that became imbedded was that I had to work hard and work long hours to make a living. The idea that I could make a lot of money wasn't even in the realm of my thinking at the time. We had people in our community who I thought were "really rich" but there was also this underlying belief that they were "greedy." So what did I learn about money? Money = Greed. And if money equaled greed, that meant that if I had money, others would judge me as greedy. Wow, I certainly didn't want THAT.

On the farm, we worked all of the time, so I learned to really love the rhythm of the farm. Of course, I grumbled when I had to bail hay, clean manure, etc., but secretly I loved how quickly I could see visible results after a day of hard work. It was a very fulfilling life in so many ways and taught me to be very disciplined. And at some level, I felt like this type of work was noble because we didn't have a lot of money. I had learned that meant I was "good" because of that.

Growing up, my parents encouraged me to go to college and get a good job. Education bore the promise of stability and perhaps an easier life—well, at least "easier" in terms of less physical labor. I attended a small liberal arts college in Minnesota, got my degree in Psychology and Communication, and figured I'd go to Law School and live happily ever after. However, there was also this underlying belief from family and community that the goal should be to work hard but not to make a lot of money, or else I would be perceived as being "greedy."

It took me many years to realize how deep those beliefs ran for me.

At the time, my belief was that I needed to make enough money to go to Law School before I could enroll. It's not a bad belief. I just didn't want to be in a ton of debt when I graduated. Looking back, I'm not sure that I really wanted to go to Law School, so perhaps my belief that I needed to have money to pay for it first kept me off that path and veering down another. In order to pay for my education, I decided to get a job in outside sales. I had done a lot of research and I learned that I could get a job in outsides sales and potentially make a lot of money.

At that time, I was working in a retail store making $6.25 per hour. Notice how that allowed me to work long hours and make very little money... and live into my Limiting Belief. I knew that wasn't going to pay for Law School, so I held tight to the belief that I could find a job in outside sales—no matter what it took. And I began to entertain the belief that maybe I, little old me, could make a lot of money. And as soon as I had that clear goal in mind and the belief that it was possible, a woman crossed my path at the retail store and invited me to interview for a position in outside sales. Bingo! It was really that easy. I interviewed, was hired, and headed down a path of complete excitement and possibility that led me to become a sales professional, sales manager, branch manager, regional manager, Executive Vice-President, and ultimately President of a multi-million-dollar technical training company in only five years.

When I started my own business, I still had some of these old beliefs running the show, which explains why even though I was intentionally using the Law of Attraction and intention to make life and business easier, it required a ton of hours and hard work. I ran myself ragged building this business the first few years, and while I'm grateful for all of the hard-earned lessons that I can now share with you, I wish I'd shifted these beliefs earlier and stepped into more of the ease I live in now. (If you have interest in learning more about that story, check out my other book, *Selling With Intention*.)

Which brings me to a topic that you probably wouldn't expect to be in a book about sales: Forgiveness.

FORGIVENESS

In order to change your beliefs about sales or money, there is usually some forgiveness involved.

Why?

Because often we've made what we believe are "mistakes" with money. So when we go out to sell more and "ask" more money to come in so we can reach our stretch goals, we can get paralyzed with old beliefs about money and our relationship with it.

Maybe you made a "bad" investment and lost a lot of money.

Maybe no one ever taught you how to handle money and you haven't learned how to save it yet, so how can you ask for more?

Maybe you don't have a plan for your money so as soon as you get it, it disappears.

Maybe you give all of your money away because you aren't sure what you'd do with it if you had a lot of it. Or perhaps you are afraid of what people will think about you if you become really wealthy.

Whatever your story and beliefs are, it's okay. I've shared many of my most Limiting Beliefs with you, and they were really painful. Acknowledging those beliefs so you can change them is going to be really important, but before you do that, *you need to forgive yourself.*

As I covered this topic in one of my Sales Camps, I could one of the participant's eyes welling up with tears. I stopped for a moment to ask her if she wanted to share. She said, with tears running down her face, "That's it! That's me! I made some bad financial decisions and I have been beating myself up for years and I KNOW it is negatively impacting my sales results!" She believed that because she had made some "bad" past decisions about money, she didn't deserve to make more money now. This was a huge breakthrough for her. Once she stopped judging herself for past decisions made, she started to cold call (which she had been deeply afraid of doing before) and suddenly had an abundance of new opportunities and a lot more joy in her business.

So give yourself a break. Give yourself some forgiveness. And let's change those beliefs!

QUANTUM CORNER

TERI JOHNSON

Keeping it Personal, LLC

http://keepingitpersonal.com

SALES CAMP CAME at THE perfect time for me. I needed a "reset," as my business was going through significant changes but I wasn't sure how I was going to navigate through them. I attended with an open mind and was ready to receive and learn whatever I needed to take my business to the next level.

On day one, Ursula said, "You get what you expect, NOT what you believe." That was powerful for me to hear and was the start of a big mindset shift for me! I had many questions swimming around in my head that were keeping me stuck. From, 'Who am I to be doing this?' to 'Is what I'm offering valuable?' and 'Could I maintain the lifestyle business and expand my business?' I learned I needed to set my intention and move forward in my business with that intention. Sales Camp and Ursula's book, *Selling With Intention,* solidified that for me and empowered me to create my 90-Day Intentional Sales Plan.

The new belief I created at Sales Camp was, "I'm offering solutions!" That is what I know now about sales and selling. It felt great to move into that New Belief Zone, because it took selling out of the equation! When I show up with that belief when connecting with a prospect, I close more sales and generate more revenue. I ask questions and I listen. When I hear their challenge, problem, or roadblock that I have a solution for, I offer it up to them! I become their person to help them solve it.

By day 2 of Sales Camp, I realized I couldn't do this alone. I needed accountability and someone to guide me, and that's when I decided to join the Synchronize Program. That was the first action step I took that made the biggest impact on my sales growth. Additionally, I got laser-focused on my One Great Goal and developed a plan or "road map" to get me there.

Consistency has been the primary practice that has helped me sync up the flow of sales and money in my business. The team I've built to support me in my efforts has been extremely valuable; we work hard and have a lot of fun along the way.

What Belief is Stopping You?

I discovered how to create belief changes at the NLP Institute of California in San Francisco. Changing beliefs was easier than I'd originally thought it would be and I was amazed by the immediate impact on my life and my results when I changed a belief.

As I mentioned earlier, beliefs are just habitual thoughts that you think are true. And since you think they are true, you keep pointing to the evidence that reinforces your beliefs. For example, during the Great Recession, I knew people who believed it was the worst time to be in business, and they struggled terribly. I also had clients who were able to shift their belief to knowing it was the best time to be in business. Because they believed it was the best time to be in business, they looked for opportunities rather than evidence that things were "bad out there." And since they were looking for opportunities, they found them. Sure, they could have believed it was the worst time to be in business too and found evidence of that. But they were willing to believe in something bigger than them.

If you want to figure out what your beliefs are that are stopping you, simply look at your results, or lack of results. For example, let's say that you aren't achieving your sales goals or you are getting mediocre results. Maybe you are only selling $12,000 per month and you really need to be selling $50,000 per month. Ask yourself, *"Why am I only selling $12,000 per month?"* and then notice the first things that come up for you. The "reasons" you are not reaching $50,000 per month will show you where you Limiting Beliefs lie. Your belief might be, *"I can't sell $50,000 per month because there aren't enough clients in my area who need what I sell."* OR, *"I can't sell $50,000 per month because even though what we have to offer is higher quality, people would rather buy the lower quality item because it costs less."* If those are your beliefs, you can see how they will stop you dead in your tracks.

Once you've identified your Limiting Belief (or beliefs), the first step is to figure out what's *not* true about it. In the example above, we can say that the following isn't true:

"I can't sell $50,000 per month because there aren't enough clients in my area who need what I sell."

While there might be some truth to this "in your area" if you live in a small town in the middle of nowhere, it might still be possible to sell outside of your area, move, etc. The key is to see what's not true so you can look at all of the possibilities.

"I can't sell $50,000 per month because even though what we have to offer is higher quality, people would rather buy the lower quality item because it costs less."

I hear this one a lot and we KNOW it's not true. People will find the money to buy something if they really want it. The key from a sales perspective is to find out WHY they really want it. What's their burning desire all about? When you know the WHY, you can then sell to that WHY and solve their problem.

Once you know what's not true about the belief, you can then begin to see all of the possibilities that exist. Seeing all of the possibilities will also allow you to see the opportunities that are right around you—and have probably been around you for a long time.

I'm going to take you through a more extensive process in the next few pages to truly release the belief. But I have just shared the basics of a belief change.

RELEASE YOUR LIMITING BELIEFS

The beliefs that you carry are influencing your behavior, which is preventing you from achieving your sales and other goals. For the purpose of this exercise, let's focus on your sales or income goal.

First, write down what you don't want regarding your sales or income goals:

(For example, you don't want to struggle every month anymore.)

_____

_____

_____

Then, write down the monthly sales goal income that you'd like to achieve:

3500 _____

_____

_____

_____

Next, write down what you believe regarding why you haven't achieved your monthly sales stretch goal:

_____

_____

_____

_____

Describe your Limiting Belief. Is it a feeling? Where is it in your body? Is it words that you hear in your head? Which ear? Whose voice? Write down whatever you notice.

_____

_____

_____

What would you do if this belief really weren't true? Who would you call? Or, what action would you take?

_____

_____

_____

What are five things that are *not* true about this belief? Write those ideas down.

_____

_____

_____

_____

_____

_____

As you think about and explore this belief, are you beginning to feel doubtful about it? Is it possible that it's not really true? Think about a time in your life when you believed something to be true and then later found out it was not. Do you remember what that felt like? Get a sense of that feeling.

_____

_____

_____

Unless we are especially lucky, most of our childhoods included the development of Limiting Beliefs. I had my fair share and I remember school being painful because I was so shy and afraid of the world. I remember feeling certain that everyone else was better-looking, better-dressed—just better in every way. But then I discovered that I loved to read and my life took off! At an early age, I learned to model successful people by reading about them, and my reading skills paid off as I excelled in school. Soon, those Limiting Beliefs turned into Achieving Beliefs, and I began to believe that what I desired might actually be possible.

ACHIEVING BELIEFS

Now that you have identified your Limiting Beliefs, I want to introduce you to the idea of Achieving Beliefs! An Achieving Belief is a belief that you have taken on as a new thought that lifts you to new levels in your life. Some people call them mantras, which can simply mean a commonly repeated word or phrase. To me, they are mantras and powerful thoughts, tied together!

EXAMPLES OF ACHIEVING BELIEFS:

▶ *I live in my Soul Purpose every day, which allows me to impact the world in unique and amazing ways!*

▶ *I am at my best when I am focused on my One Great Goal and significantly impacting the lives of others!*

▶ *Money flows to me effortlessly, and I receive all of the gifts from the Universe!*

Your goal should be to get your Achieving Beliefs into "the muscle" by repeating them over and over again, so post them somewhere you will see them multiple times per day. When they feel like natural thoughts, you will know that they have become part of your subconscious, which will naturally impact your ability to more easily attract the success you desire. This, coupled with your focus on your One Great Goal, will make it even easier to allow your goals to easily come to you.

Years ago, I was working with belief changes in my *3-Day Selling With Intention Intensive* courses. One of the women in class had created a new belief for herself but right before the belief change process, she raised her hand and motioned for me to come over. She said that the Achieving Belief that she had created did not resonate with her. That meant, at a deep level, she intuitively felt like something wasn't right or that something wasn't working. We changed a few words and she kept saying it out loud until it resonated with her body, mind, and spirit. I could see exactly when that occurred because all of the stress was erased from her face and a look of peace came over her. She stated her Achieving Belief out loud again, this time confidently, and every person in the room could hear the difference.

When you are taking on a new belief, try it on and say it aloud until you feel at a deep level that it is true. You will know because you will feel peaceful, and it will just work for you.

I heard back from this woman the following week. She was thrilled to report that without doing anything except repeating her new Achieving Belief, she had received calls from nine new clients! NINE! She then told me she was CERTAIN that her new Achieving Belief was working for her. I'd say!

Choose your Achieving Beliefs carefully and make sure they resonate with your Soul!

Ask yourself this, "What belief would better serve my life or business?" How would you state this new belief? Write it down in the present tense and be specific!

Example

Old Belief: I don't have what it takes to be a successful speaker.

New Belief: I am a successful speaker who easily attracts and delivers five high-paying speaking engagements every month.

Old Belief

_____

_____

_____

New Belief

I attract quality clients and money flows easily to me as I meet and exceed their expectations while bringing them peace of mind both in their finances.

Do you now sense that this belief is becoming true for you? Are you open to taking on this new belief and keeping the old belief filed away? Think back to a time when you took on a new belief—you may not have totally accepted it, but you were open to the new possibility. What three things will be different in your personal and professional life when you take on this new belief? Write those three things down.

_____

_____

_____

Sometimes old nagging beliefs about money will raise their ugly heads. But I continue to challenge them and choose new beliefs that support the steps I am taking in my life. I used to believe that you have to work hard, physically hard, to make money. It took me years to release that belief and recognize that "Making money is fun and easy!" And so it is!

A POWERFUL VISUALIZATION TECHNIQUE

When my clients attend Sales Camp, I walk them through this powerful visualization process that I have adapted from my training at the NLP Institute of California. Walk yourself through this process to fully release your old Limiting Beliefs.

Visualization: Close your eyes. Imagine that you are at your bank and that you have a special safety deposit box for all of your old beliefs. See yourself opening up the safety deposit box, putting the old beliefs in, and locking them away. Recognize that you can pull the old belief out any time and read it, but it will remain safely in the safety deposit box. Take a deep breathe in and relax, knowing that you have released this old belief.

What do you feel like?

_____

_____

_____

Now, close your eyes. Imagine it is six months from today. In your visualization, you have taken on your new belief and you are imagining your future. Perhaps you are celebrating with family or friends. Wherever you are, just imagine that the colors are really bright and be in the moment. Rather than observing yourself, imagine that you are there in the moment experiencing everything that is happening. Notice the sounds you hear around you. Notice the smells that are floating by. Now, even more importantly, imagine how great it feels in your core, or stomach area, to achieve this goal. Whatever you are feeling, multiply that feeling by ten. Breathe in how awesome you feel!

Then, imagine that there is a timeline in front of you that goes all the way back to the day you did the visualization six months earlier. On that timeline, notice how things came together for you easily and gracefully as soon as you took on this new belief. Notice what you let go of (the old belief) and anything else that made your journey easier. One more time, breathe into this great feeling of living without this old belief! Notice how awesome you feel!

Once the new belief is established, it is important that the new belief stay. To do that, I recommend writing it down in your day timer on each day, for the next six months.

Remember, beliefs were created because they served you in some way in the past. They might have even protected you. But now it seems that you are ready to let go of this belief because it no longer serves you and is now interfering with your business and your life.

Release Your Fear

Fear can stop the best of us and it can also lower our frequency. It can creep up on us when we least expect it. It catches us off-guard when we definitely don't need it, and it can take us out of our game. Fear develops from the thought that we are going to lose something, so we have to hold on to it. When we are afraid of losing something, it means that we believe that there will never be more or there will never be enough. Often times, those types of fears are rooted in our childhood and the way we were raised.

You can identify fears by observing your own behavior or having someone else give you feedback about your behavior. For example, you might avoid public speaking opportunities at all costs. This is a behavior. To identify the fear behind the behavior, ask yourself why you avoid those types of opportunities. *"I avoid public speaking because if I screw up, people might laugh at me."* Fears and beliefs go hand in hand because most of the time, fears are rooted in a belief.

Think about the impact of your fears on your success right now. How has fear prevented you from reaching your goals? List five goals that you haven't reached due to fear or avoidant behavior.

1. _____
2. _____
3. _____
4. _____
5. _____

I am going to share an exercise with you to allow you to release fear. One of the things I have discovered about fear is that people often carry the feeling of fear around with them. It is very physical, and it causes physical problems. When you release a fear, you will usually notice immediate relief in your body. Releasing a fear is like releasing old energy that has been holding on for a long time. When you release it, you will also be making room for new opportunities and positive energy to come in!

Example:

Fear: I am afraid that I won't succeed.

What You Really Want: To move through each day with peace and confidence that I am on my way to achieving my One Great Goal!

Fear

_____

_____

_____

What You Really Want

_____

_____

_____

Before I share this fear release exercise, I want to encourage you to pay attention to your feelings as you go through it. For many people, this exercise will take them to the next level immediately. Others will have to complete the exercise several times. And still others may need the support of a friend or even therapist because of the intensity of the fears they are dealing with. If you feel so much resistance that it is affecting you physically to even read *about* this exercise, please find someone to support you as you work to release your fears.

FEAR RELEASE EXERCISE

Close your eyes. Take a deep breath in through your nose and then release it through your mouth. Think about your fear. Notice where you feel it in your body. Maybe you feel it in your stomach. Maybe you feel it in your shoulders. Just notice it.

Where do you feel it?

_____

_____

_____

Then, in your mind's eye, imagine what this fear looks like. Notice the shape. Does it look like an arrow, a blob, or a circle? Notice the color. Then notice how it makes you feel. Whatever you are feeling, increase it, so you are really clear on what it is you want to release.

What does it look like? How does it feel?

_____

_____

_____

Next, remember that this fear kept you safe in some way. Acknowledge how it did and silently give thanks for that gift. Realize, though, that this fear no longer serves you and is actually holding you back from reaching your One Great Goal.

Explain how that fear kept you safe. Thank it.

_____

_____

_____

Now give yourself permission to let it go by closing your eyes and imagining that it can leave your body and move into your hands. Once it is in your hands, keeping your eyes closed, imagine that it grows wings; and when you are ready, throw it up into the air and watch it fly away into the sun until you can no longer "see" it. Trust that it is gone—it is released.

BONUS BELIEF CHANGE PROCESS

Okay, so you've taken yourself through a belief change process as well as a fear release exercise, but perhaps you still feel like something is still a little stuck. That's okay! I'd like to share another NLP based process that can help you eradicate whatever is left of those old beliefs and fears.

This is another great process to help you achieve your desired sales goals. Perhaps your Limiting Belief about selling enough is actually tied to not having enough money, or not believing you could make enough money.

Think about your Limiting Belief around money (not having enough). Now, remember what happened to you as a child and watch it in your mind as if it is a movie on a TV screen. Now make it black and white. Then, imagine that the movie keeps getting smaller and smaller in your mind and hold it at a distance until it's a little bit fuzzy. If there is sound, let it be very, very quiet.

Then, speed the movie up super-fast and replay it a few times. The movie should play out like you are fast-forwarding it.

Next, run the movie backwards in your mind at least 4 times in a row. And then just release it—let it go.

Now, create a new movie in your mind with your new belief. See yourself having more than enough money, enjoying time off, enjoying hobbies, having a wonderful relationship, having fun, etc. See the movie in black and white and then gradually change it to color. Then, run it forward slowly and then at normal speed.

Then, rather than watching the movie, actually imagine yourself stepping into it, as if it's happening to you and you are enjoying more than enough money, time off, hobbies, a relationship, having fun, etc. Engage all of your senses and be in the moment of fun and joy.

Finally, think of something unrelated (like washing your laundry) and then think back to the old belief. It shouldn't carry any emotion for you anymore.

Think of your new belief again and what your life will be like. My guess is that you have great positive emotion connected to it!

FAITH CHANGES EVERYTHING

Shifting your beliefs involves a lot of faith. You have to believe at some level that what you desire is possible. It's available. It's out there. If you can just grab onto a little bit of that belief you can move from 10% to 20% and then on to 50% and then to 75% until you can eek your way to 95% in belief creation. Interestingly, I've learned that if you can get to at least 80%, you begin to hit a bit of a tipping point. It's as if the Universe begins to hear your drum banging and the evidence of your goal coming into manifestation begins to show up in weird and wonky ways.

Let me give you an example. At the beginning of 2013, I was at a Vision Board workshop given by an amazing, intuitive friend of mine (YES, I surround myself with a lot of intuitive people!). She had a special way of doing vision boards because after we put ours together, then she would "read" it for deeper meaning.

When she "read" mine, she told me that I would be pregnant soon and that a baby was on the way.

I was too invested with hope in that belief to even dare believe it was possible. I left kind of huffy, and I'll admit, I felt angry because I was scared of getting bad news. But I didn't realize that my belief had already tipped the 95% point months before.

When I left the Vision Board class that day, I had a thought: What if I am actually pregnant right now?

The next day, I was at the Dollar Store buying some cool party stuff. (I already told you—I can be a little frugal!).On a whim, I picked up a pregnancy test for a dollar. (Yes, they sell those there!)

I took it home and used it. It said I was pregnant.

My heart stopped and I thought, "Well, that thing can't be right because I only paid $1 for it!"

I drove to the local CVS and picked up two of the most expensive pregnancy tests they had and took them home. They were, of course, both positive.

Shifting was the first step for me. Pregnancy and a move across the country quickly followed!

QUANTUM CORNER

JENNIFER I. BUCHHOLZ

Transform via Travel

www.transformviatravel.com

S ALES CAMP ENABLED me to launch a business from scratch and that business is now 18 months old and still in the growth and building stage. In the meantime, to fund that endeavor, I applied the concepts to my other entrepreneurial endeavor, and with the skills and strategic effort learned at Sales Camp, I'm on track to quadruple my sales this year.

Before Sales Camp, I had zero confidence about sales. I abhorred the idea of being a sales person and that kept me from being successful. I knew I needed to learn a sales approach that would feel authentic to me. When I started Sales Camp, I barely knew what I was going to sell or how I was going to do it.

I love the OGG process. My first time at Sales Camp, I wanted to compile an anthology of solo women's travel stories and my book was my OGG. I adjusted the goal a bit to better position myself as the SME (small to medium enterprise) and wrote the book and hit Amazon #1 bestseller within 9 months of setting that OGG. The practices that help me the most is writing down 5 daily gratitudes and 5 daily accomplishments.

Before Sales Camp, I believed sales people were smarmy

and slick and were more about the sales than the delivery. I also believed that I could not sell—I did not have the desire or the skills. I was comfortable consulting, but I didn't have the skills or abilities to close a deal.

Since Sales Camp, I moved into a New Belief Zone and I believed that not only could I sell, but that I have people who need what I have to offer. If I don't sell to them, they might not get what they need. This new belief helped me because I was no longer afraid to sell. Instead, I felt compelled to help. It was just like flipping a switch in my brain.

The actions that I take that make the biggest impact on my sales growth include sharing what I do, asking just for the next step, and following up. Now, I KNOW that I got this. I can sell what I believe in and people want to buy it. I also know that I am capable of creating the company, schedule, and life of my dreams!

STEP #5: ACT

"Once you make a decision, the universe conspires to make it happen."

~ Ralph Waldo Emerson ~

I STOPPED ABRUPTLY at the door when I saw them. My mom and my newborn, Lucca, rocking peacefully in the chair. The sight brought tears to my eyes, as I thought about all of the years that I wondered if I could have a baby—all the years I longed to see my mom snuggle a child of mine.

And today, she has to go home.

She'd flown out from Minnesota to help us for the first week, and the two of them had bonded from the moment they laid eyes on each other. Magically, she had landed exactly 3 hours before Lucca was born because he was a week late! He was literally waiting for my Mom to arrive.

This isn't enough time. She shouldn't live across the country from him. I want him to be close to her—to be close to our whole family. What's it going to take for us to get our butts to Minnesota? We have to do this soon—for Lucca, for Mom, for all of us.

I shared my decision with Tim on the way back from the airport, and he nodded in agreement and reached over to squeeze my hand in solidarity. "I know, Urs. I feel it too. I just don't see how yet."

A few weeks later, he came home from work a little early one day with this look in his eye that said, "I'm done." Something had happened at work and it made him realize that his time there was coming to a close. He had accomplished everything he had desired to accomplish at that company and he felt things coming to a natural end.

We had waffled for such a long time. Should we move back? Should we stay? Tim and I had written countless pro/con lists regarding moving back to Minnesota that went something like this:

Pros:

Be close to family

Cons:

Less opportunity

Cold weather

And that was about all we could come up with. So, we didn't move.

But when he walked in the door that day, I knew something had shifted. "How soon will you be completely done?" I asked, my heart beginning to race under the warmth of our newborn's little body.

"Now."

That was it. The gavel had dropped. The decision had been made. So together, our collective intention got "all in." He didn't resign that day, but he did send out resumes and set up interviews.

A week later, he resigned because he had an incredible job offer in Minnesota.

And, within two weeks, we moved. Yep, you read that right. Two weeks.

DECIDING MEANS YOU ARE ALL IN

For the first time, Tim and I were ALL IN and taking action at the same time. No more resistance. No more inner conflict. No more pros and cons lists.

We decided. We started acting as if it was going to happen. That was it. Minnesota was where we needed to be, and so everything started to move in that direction at quantum speed.

Of course, I wanted time to tell my clients we were leaving. I wanted to connect with my dearest friends. I wanted a moment. But when you DECIDE and commit and step into a New Belief Zone, heaven and earth begins to move on your behalf.

Within two weeks, we had packed up and taken a road trip with our six-month-old son, Lucca, across the western United States to move back to my home state.

QUANTUM COLLAPSE

Right before a decision comes waffling. Do I want this? Do I not want this? In Quantum Physics, we learn about the Observer Effect. Simply put, things that we observe change when we look at them. The art of observing something changes it. YES, science has made this discovery and yet we are all still wondering how to achieve our goals!

If you want to impact your current situation, you must decide and get all in. No waffling. No backup plan. You decide that no matter what, you will write that book. No matter what, you will start that business.

I heard a scientist say that when we observe the goal we want and choose it, it collapses all other possibilities in the quantum field. Think about that! There are all of these possible paths and outcomes floating around you all the time, tugging you in multiple directions, making you waffle. But when you choose, it's as if every other possibility falls away... and the one you've chosen is able to receive all of your intention and energy. And it doesn't have to fight through other possibilities on its way to you either!

Ralph Waldo Emerson wrote that once you make a decision, the Universe conspires to make it happen. The Universe Conspires! I have seen this happen repeatedly once I have made a decision and gotten all in with my desired goal. I meet the perfect person to help me take the next step. The right opportunity shows up that will be the vehicle to take me to the goal. I know that my job isn't to get all caught up in how it will all unfold. My job is to take the next step that is right in front of me.

And, sometimes, a decision requires some change of habits in order to sustain your intention—to take action and continue your momentum.

COMMITMENT, NEW ACTION, AND HABITS

Whenever we make a change in our lives, it takes commitment. We have to decide that we are going to follow our dreams and goals regardless of what it takes to make change happen (inside of our values, of course!), even it if is outside of our Comfort

Zone... and outside of our current Belief Zone. Once you have the found the Clarity of your One Great Goal, written your goals down, synced up your frequency with what you want, and shifted your beliefs, then it's time to get committed and create new habits in your life to allow the goal to more easily come to fruition, which makes it easier to continue to take action. Later in this chapter, I will use the example of sales to show you how it's possible. The truth is, if you cannot make it a habit, you will not continue to take action and you will find yourself back in your Comfort Zone, facing your old results.

When my husband and I decided to take on a rigorous new workout, it took a ton of commitment on our parts. First, we had to study a lot of the weight lifting moves so we could understand how to do them without hurting ourselves. (Okay, well, he studied them and then showed me.) We engaged with a system called Workout Box because we appreciated their videos and simple explanations. Then, we jumped into the program and decided to work out a minimum of 4-5 times per week. We worked out during the evenings and on the weekends as well. I'm a morning person, so the evening workouts were way outside of my Comfort Zone. My body would be thinking about going to bed and instead we'd be down in the workout facility lifting weights and running. It was tough to stay committed to this program, but by supporting each other and by staying on track for a few weeks, this new commitment became a habit for us.

Sales habits are exactly the same. Take a look at your revised Sales Goal again and let's discover how you can develop new sales habits to make this goal a reality.

Having been a sales professional, executive, president of a multimillion-dollar company, sales trainer and coach, I am often asked what it REALLY takes to be successful in sales. And while clear intention and knowing the right sales strategies is extremely important, it's just as important to develop powerful sales habits that allow you to create and sustain your sales success.

Too often, I see people attend all kinds of training seminars, get super excited about what they just learned, only to return to their office without having changed any "bad" sales habits for the long haul. That's the exact reason why I am committed to sales training sessions that integrate experiential learning because once you've experienced it and gotten it "in the muscle," you have the skills to begin building new sales habits.

A habit is simply an automatic behavior, or a behavior that you don't have to think about. A bad sales habit would be not following up with your prospects. A good sales habit would be having time on your calendar every week to make follow-up sales calls. (Argh! I feel you cringing!)

Research shows that when you change one habit, it can positively impact other areas of your life—the domino effect. It also shows that it might be easier, and faster, to change a bad habit than once thought. There is some work I recently came across that reveals exactly what we need to know about changing bad habits to good ones, and tools to make it happen more quickly. First, there is Charles Duhigg's book *The Power of Habit*, in which he demonstrates the science of habit formation in depth and teaches us how habits are formed and what we can do to change them. And second, there is a gentleman named B.J. Fogg, whose body of work partially focuses on how long it takes for someone to change a habit. He has a program called *3 Tiny Habits*, which basically shows that by tying a new habit to an existing habit, you can change a habit in as little as one week. Don't underestimate the power of this method simply because of its simplicity. The brilliance behind it is that he is tying the new habit to something we are already doing, which makes it easier to insert the new behavior.

From a bad habit perspective, let's use smoking as an example. My mom smoked for 35 years. After I attended the NLP Institute of California, I came away with a toolbox filled with tools to help her quit (which she did). One of the main things she needed to do was to change the habit loop. For my mom, cigarettes were her self-described "best friend." They got her through the good times and the bad times and every time in between. Essentially, whenever she felt any kind of emotion, or just wanted to bond with her husband and friends, she grabbed a cigarette. As much as the nicotine had a hold on her, so did the habit.

We utilized a variety of NLP techniques to help her quit smoking, including belief change and visualization processes. All of them helped. But once she inserted a new routine and reward into her loop—something that Duhigg discusses in length and refers to as *Cue, Routine, and then Reward*—she was able to create the habit of staying quit. It's one thing to quit a habit; it's another thing to "stay quit." When my mom would feel the urge to grab a cigarette (the cue), she would grab a piece of hard candy or even a stuffed straw to suck on (the routine) and then she would feel better (the reward). Maybe not as great as she thought she felt before, but her emotions improved enough to create a new habit.

So that's how you change a habit and build the discipline you need to reach your goals. One of the new habits she added that improved her overall health was walking every day. The mornings were hardest for her so when she wanted to have that first cigarette, she went for a walk instead. She always had coffee or hot tea in the morning, so she tied her new walking habit to that one. She would have her hot beverage and then head out for her walk. According to Fogg's work, that's the fastest and easiest way to create a new habit—simply tie it to an existing one.

I use my mom quitting smoking as an example because she utilized these ideas to change a really tough habit. By seeing how she was able to do it, I want to encourage YOU to kick a bad sales habit because it will be even easier for you.

I have worked with many clients who wanted to add a new habit of making regular sales calls to their schedule. But no matter what they did, the just couldn't make it happen. Can you relate? They tried scheduling them early. They tried scheduling them late in the day. They even tried scheduling them at lunch, but nothing seemed to work.

Why?

Because they hadn't created a new habit. Instead, they were *trying* to make it happen. Notice that the word *try* makes you always feel like you are striving for something but never arrive? You need to make the decision to create a new habit and then it can change.

Let's apply Fogg's work to the sales goal example to create a new sales habit.

STEPS TO KICK A BAD HABIT AND INSERT A NEW ONE:

1. First, identify the bad habit you want to change. Example: *Not following up with prospects.*

2. Then, decide that you are going to create a new sales habit. Example: *You want to begin following up regularly with your prospects to set appointments.*

3. Next, identify an existing habit you can tie it to. Example: *Every morning, without fail, you check your email immediately when you come into the office.*

4. Decide how to shift the habit: Example: *To kick the bad habit and insert the new habit, give yourself 20 minutes to check your email and then immediately go into 30-60 minutes of follow-up calls.*

5. Follow through every day until you know it is an established new habit. Example: *Add it to your calendar for the rest of the year!*

Imagine what will happen to your sales results simply by having this new habit. If you have an off day and things don't go as planned, don't give up. Simply go back to your behavior. After all, there will be days when things don't go as planned, but it doesn't mean that your new habit hasn't become automatic. Brushing your teeth is probably an automatic habit, but there might be a day or two during the year when you might just be so exhausted that you fall into bed with teeth that aren't perfectly clean. And you even survive!

Take the time to go through the steps today so you can create powerful habits for tomorrow.

Once you've decided to kick an old sales habit that isn't serving you, then you can open up to creating new sales habits that will allow you to commit to the change you desire.

QUANTUM CORNER

Renee Frey

TalentQ, Inc.

www.talentq.net

As a result of Sales Camp and then Synchronize, TalentQ has achieved a 311% increase in sales! DYNAMITE! When I decided to attend Sales Camp, I needed clarity about tactics for business development. I wanted to keep up with the fast growth of my company and needed some guidance on how to do this most in the most effective way.

My biggest discovery through this process was learning that my goal *was* attainable. When I first wrote my goal down, it seemed daunting! After what I learned at Sales Camp, my mindset changed. My One Great Goal, to triple my business, was within reach and I was able to accomplish it!

The main new habit that helped me the most is to always be looking at the data and the pipeline of potential sales. Analyzing data has helped me to focus my attention exactly where it needs to be to best benefit TalentQ, Inc.

Before Sales Camp and Synchronize, I believed that I was bothering people when I reached out to them. Looking back, WOW! Was that REALLY limiting me! Now I believe that everyone is waiting for my phone call. TalentQ has excellent services to offer and standing firm in that truth reaps awesome results.

I used to believe that I didn't deserve the money I was receiving, even though I was working hard and offering an outstanding service. Now, I feel empowered because I believe I am worthy of all of the money that flows to me. That new belief has helped me double my sales, because I believe everyone is waiting for my call! My new beliefs have made me the top sales person at TalentQ, Inc., because I have confidence in myself and the strength of my business.

The regular actions that I take that have made the most impact are: First, I set intentions with each phone call, because setting "next steps" and giving people specific times you're available next will show results; then I track metrics, because it's important to *always* know your numbers; and finally, I hired a team because I realized that I can't do it all alone.

Now, as the top sales person at TalentQ, Inc., I know that I actually enjoy sales and selling. I have also received compliments on my leadership capabilities after people meet my AWESOME team! I now believe that I am capable of creating a multimillion-dollar recruiting firm and my New Belief Zone includes a KNOWING that I can accomplish any dynamite goal I can think of!

DISCIPLINE

Once you have created new habits, it is up to you to have the discipline to do what you committed to do and to take action on your goals every day. My clients often ask me what my "secrets" are and which "special habits" I have developed along the way that help me reach my goals. The truth is that there aren't any secrets, but I am disciplined in following through on the habits that I create. I take action every day. Discipline is defined as *"the state of improved behavior, etc., resulting from such training or conditions"* according to Collins English Dictionary. In other words, as you train yourself to have better habits, your behavior improves and ultimately your results improve. Just like Tiger Woods and other accomplished professionals and athletes, we need to work with coaches and mentors who will train us to create new habits that actually work. They will also help us break through blocks that might otherwise have stopped us.

But when it is just us, sitting at our computer alone, it is up to us to keep going and do the work, which can be the hardest part. This is where you must have other practices to help you feel like you can take another step forward even when you don't want to. One of my favorite books is *Eat that Frog* by Brian Tracy. He shows you how to do the thing you least want to do first (like making sales calls) to get your day launched right. I follow this principle and I'm always amazed by how much work I get done by starting with "the frog."

My other core personal practices include working with healers, yoga, meditation, reading spiritual works, and prayer.

The key is to discover what that "thing" is for you that will keep you motivated when you are stuck. Is it a reward? Is it knowing that you will have time off? Is it the satisfaction of finishing something? Whatever it is, keep the end in mind and stay focused there so you remember why you have set the goals that you set.

Decision, Action, and Discipline Lead to Powerful Rewards

Napoleon Hill directs us to, "Conduct yourself just as you would if you were already in possession of the material thing which you are demanding when you call upon your subconscious mind." Act as if it is already here.

After we made the decision to move back to Minnesota, and I decided to make Sales Coach Now a national brand, I grew my team and the support I needed to make that happen... BEFORE I had the business that would require that team.

I want to make sure you don't miss what I just said.

I decided I wanted Sales Coach Now to become a national brand and change people's lives all over the United States. I took the action of building the team and the model for the business that I was creating next, not the one I had then. And then I stayed focused and disciplined in the sales habits that were working for me.

Pretty soon, not only had I doubled my revenue, but I had created a life that had the support available for me to do other things I really wanted to do—like take a Mediterranean cruise with my family for two weeks. As I ate pasta in Italy and walked the shores of Croatia, I marveled at my life and this whole goal achievement process.

Until we make a decision and take action in alignment with it, it really is as if we have one foot in the universe we've been living in and one foot in the universe that is full of more possibility, more profit, and more play.

Once we make a decision and begin to move into a New Belief Zone, take the next steps that start to unfold in front of us really quickly, and make decisions based on what's coming (not what we see un front of us), a whole new world opens up for us... literally. But we have to take action!

In other words, if you want to grow a million-dollar business, you must start thinking like a million-dollar business owner. Stand in those NEW shoes—that New Belief Zone—and make your decisions from THAT place.

QUANTUM CORNER

DENISE LEVINE

Outside In Organizer and Makeovers

www.outsideinorganizer.com

MY LIMITING BELIEFS resulted in my waking up worrying about money. I focused on how to spend less until I could make more. I wouldn't say that this was my "Comfort Zone" because I was less than comfortable. Rather, I would call it my "Frozen Zone." I was stuck in these thoughts based on fear and scarcity. I was working long hours every day and still not getting my desired results.

When I stretched into a New Belief Zone, made the commitment to the program, and let go of fear, everything changed! I changed my beliefs into:

- ▶ I am capable and worthy of generating a limitless income.
- ▶ I love my work and can balance it with time for personally fulfilling activities.
- ▶ My clients value my services and willingly pay for them.

The results? Within weeks, everything shifted. I increased my prices and expanded my services. New clients signed on and current clients renewed at these new prices. In fact, I was able to exceed my sales goal within a month and a half by ree times the amount. I was sleeping better and made time to include more personal activities with friends. Eventually, my sales doubled!

The thing I needed clarity most on was the best closing strategies because before I attended Sales Camp, I had a Limiting Belief that I would not have enough money to support myself because selling was limited and difficult. After Sales Camp, I discovered that selling can be fun and that I owe it to my potential clients to follow up with them! That new belief built my confidence and led to me doubling my sales. The actions that made the biggest impact on my sales were consistent follow up, offering my biggest package first, and asking for what I want (leads, etc.). My biggest knowing NOW is that I am actually good at sales and I am capable of creating a successful business and a balanced life.

This was my best year yet. And I am so excited about next year and all of the possibilities. My goals are bigger and completely aligned with my New Belief Zone.

Step #6: Know

"High expectations are the key to everything."

~ Sam Walton ~

As we drove across country, a part of me felt utter relief and the other part wanted to scream, "Wait! I'm not ready for this! I can't be moving back! What if this doesn't work out for us? What if we regret it?"

We crossed the Minnesota border on a day I will never forget: April 13th, 2014—my 40th birthday—and drove straight to my extended family's Easter Celebration (technically, it was Palm Sunday) where I found a room full of black balloons to help me "celebrate."

As I connected and conversed with my family that afternoon, I relaxed into the deep knowing that we had done the right thing for our family. Lucca was going to be raised by a village of people who loved him, and Tim and I would have the support we needed.

But what about the business? I thought to myself as I watched my mom kissing the sweet little infant in Tim's arms. *Was this the right thing for my business and all of those goals? Is it possible to do this here?*

Tim looked up at me and smiled, as if to answer the question.

Okay. I know. It's all going to be okay. I smiled back.

But the truth is that it wasn't until my second Sales Camp in Minnesota that I KNEW, in my core, that our move had been a success and all of our goals were going to be checked off faster than I could have imagined.

THE KNOWING

What just happened?

I was standing in front of a Sales Camp classroom (my company's signature 2-day sales training course), looking out at a packed room—and I mean, PACKED! We had just sold out all of our Synchronize Coaching spots to clients who were not part of our Top 20%. No, they were part of our Top 10%. *Well, I guess that settles it. This is exactly the right place for me and my family and my business.*

As I celebrated with my little family and my Sales Coach Now team over dinner, I realized that all of my values were totally in alignment... and how right it felt that my personal and professional life overlapped and became one.

How could this possibly get any better?

I didn't know how, but I KNEW it would.

THE LAW OF VELOCITY

Synchronicities started to explode. I had more speaking engagements (10 in one month!) and invitations than I could handle. My opportunities in California seemed to expand even though I was no longer there. It was as if my lack of local availability made me, as my friend Kim loves to say, "In demand."

Minnesotans made me feel more welcomed than I could have imagined. My very first Minnesota client, Tena, was so enthusiastic about what I was doing for my clients that she told everyone she could (she's one of those amazing givers) and purchased copies of my book, *One Great Goal*, by the case. She opened up countless doors for me and then it just continued to happen.

And then Colorado opened up. And Arizona. And Wisconsin. And Illinois.

The downside was that I was traveling more than I ever had, which created a strong inner conflict because I didn't want to be away from Lucca and Tim. But my amazing husband made it all okay. In fact, Tim made me realize that when I traveled, he actually got to bond with Lucca more than when I was around. His support meant the world. It always has.

I continued to write my goal and task checklist every day. I continued to check goals off of my Expected Goal List, and one day I just realized that I was in a completely New Belief Zone. Not only was I in it, I was living it.

How did I know I was living it? I knew it because I was beginning to experience almost instant creation. Things that would have taken me years to accomplish in the past were happening in weeks and days... or in moments. There were times when it almost frightened me because my thoughts were creating so quickly.

It wasn't just me. Tim was also experiencing instant, or almost instant, creations in his career and also in other aspects related to finances, travel, and more. Plus, the more we talked about our Belief Zone and everything that was happening, the more it happened. Our collective intention was even more powerful than our individual intentions.

I love Lynn McTaggart and Pam Grout's work. Lynn's books are about the intense research she has done in the area of intention and group intention. Pam's research focuses on the readers doing mini experiments in their own lives to discover the power of their thoughts on their results. The late, and amazingly powerful, Dr. Wayne Dyer wrote about intention in his bestseller, *The Power of Intention* (which was actually my inspiration for *Selling With Intention*). All of these prove that the clearer our intentions became, the faster our creations show up.

Of course, there is Greg Kuhn's work, which I've already shared with you. When I read his book and how he impressed upon his readers the power of expectation, it changed my life. It was more than just intention. It was more than just beliefs. Getting into The Belief Zone, I realized, was about giving ourselves permission to expect great things to happen to us.

And so, I finally gave myself permission to expect great things.

I am worth it.

You Get What You Expect

When I was a child, I loved Christmas. I still do! I loved writing my Christmas list out for Santa and waiting with anticipation to see if I would receive everything I had asked for on my list, or if perhaps I hadn't behaved well enough to receive the gifts I asked for. In any case, the belief that Santa Clause was coming to town was strong within me. It was so strong that not only did I believe, I also expected Santa to eat the cookies, drink the milk, fill the stockings, and leave all of the presents under the tree. And he did!

Years later, on Christmas Eve, one of my nephews was preparing for Santa to come with great anticipation and expectation. I could feel his excitement and it fueled my Christmas Spirit as well. The next morning, after we all woke up to see our stockings full and the gifts from Santa under the tree, my nephew mentioned that he had heard the footsteps of the reindeer on the roof when the sleigh landed. His belief and expectations were so strong that he even thought he had heard the evidence of Santa arriving.

Think about that for a moment. Think about your beliefs about money, business, and life. How do your beliefs impact what you expect will happen on a monthly basis? If you believe that money is difficult to come by, then of course this will impact how much money you expect to make and see in your bank account. If you believe that selling is difficult, then you most likely won't expect to close very many sales that month.

Your beliefs and expectations hold your reality together. Your Limiting Beliefs create blind spots in your subconscious, so even if you create a new goal that you really desire, a Limiting Belief might creep up and block your expectations.

QUANTUM CORNER

CATHY PLOTNICK

Steeped Tea Independent Consultant

www.MySteepedTeaParty.com/TheParTeaLady

AFTER ATTENDING Sales Camp for the first time, I doubled my sales and hit my quantum goal: #1 US Sales! The biggest piece of clarity that I needed from Sales Camp was how to connect with customers/team members. I lacked confidence and wasn't an achiever, so setting the quantum goal to be #1 was scary! I was afraid to step outside the box and let go of all those negative thoughts and Limiting Beliefs that stopped me.

My greatest discovery was my top 3 to 5 were all linked and together would help me achieve my One Great Goal of #1 US Sales. I had a hard time at first figuring out how to be part of the top 10. Being a goal-setter was WAY out of my Comfort Zone.

The habit and practice that helped me the most was realizing that "the fortune is in the follow-up." I am far more confident and I set the intention to earn every Steeped Tea Incentive... and I have. I am more cognizant of time I need to spend with my husband. Positive thinking has been a Godsend. I am amazed by what can happen by focusing on what I can do, rather than what I can't do... and what I am, rather than what I am not.

When I first arrived at Sales Camp, I believed that I couldn't do it. I couldn't reach my sales goals, much less be #1. No way could I, Cathy Plotnick, be #1 in the entire country. No way could I embrace fear. No way could I be an example to other Steeped Tea Consultants. ... But then it all happened!

Before Sales Camp, I believed I was marginal. I couldn't be a top seller and recruiter in the country and earn fabulous trips. I didn't think I was a good leader for my team. I struggled with relating to my team and getting them motivated. Once I learned what I needed to do, I had a clear plan on how to achieve my goal.

The new belief that I created at Sales Camp was I AM #1 and I can achieve anything I set my mind to, and any goals I focus on. It felt incredibly liberating. It was like five decades of weight lifted off my shoulders. I was so caught up in "I can't do that" that I didn't try to see if I could. I am far more confident now. I was nervous about speaking in front of people and spoke to 450 people at my conference last year. Head office trusted me and saw my promise to be a speaker at our conference. NEVER in my wildest dreams did I see myself as an example to others. I still get compliments from other consultants 9 months later on how my speech moved people. I have learned to see in myself what so many see in me.

This new belief that I adopted was the #NeverGiveUp mantra. I watched my numbers religiously and offered tea and hosting to as many people as possible. I shed the fear of being pushy when I'm just sharing the opportunity to try our tea. I learned when people know you are shooting for something big, they are more than willing to help you. I told people all the time what I was going for and they helped a lot! I needed $700 in sales in two days to hit my goal... I knew a $5k month would solidify #1 and I hit it in 6 months. My sales crept up each month to hit that golden number and my One Great Goal.

The three actions that made the most impact on my sales were that I picked up the phone to follow up, I believed in myself by adopting positive self-talk, and set the intention every day that I will do something to get me closer to my goal—give out samples, go to a new networking group, or speak in front of my City Council about my business. I did everything I could to get the word out about Steeped Tea, me, and my goal.

After shifting my belief at Sales Camp, I now KNOW that I solve a problem for people. Picking up the phone to follow up or offering the product is not pushy. Many times people are waiting for me to call and are grateful that I did. It can take many calls to get the sale, lots of no's or lack of return calls; but until I'm told "NO, never call me again," I keep calling on a regular basis to follow up and offer them my service to solve their problem.

Now, in my New Belief Zone, I know that I can be part of the MILLION-DOLLAR CLUB! I know that I will be promoted to Executive Director... I am only two steps away. It is non-negotiable I will go on every incentive trip. I am going to Rome in September after already being in Jamaica and Maui. I am 4 team members away from 100. I am capable of doing anything I set the intention to do. It is a DONE DEAL.

IT'S TIME TO EXPECT MORE

Once you've released your Limiting Beliefs, as you did in a previous chapter, it's time to give yourself permission to expect more. You cannot achieve your dream goals if you don't expect them to happen.

Expectation is like a muscle. You can build your power of expectation over time by practicing with small things first. For example, I like to expect things to be really easy when I travel and, consequently, I regularly receive free upgrades—almost always these days. I don't have to even ask for them. I just expect them to happen. And BAM, they do. Tim and I were recently flying coach on Sun Country airlines when they called me to the ticket counter. Of course, they upgraded all three of us to first class. It was worth almost five hundred dollars and we hadn't even asked! In fact, the day before I had considered paying for the upgrade but then thought I better not because there weren't seats all together. When we were upgraded, Lucca and I sat together and, magically, Tim was right across the aisle.

I love receiving these small miracles and gifts along my travels that delight me and keep me in the flow. Plus, it strengthens my belief and expectation that things really CAN be easy and that all of my goals are coming to me now. And the more I expect to see these small miracles and gifts, the more they start to show up.

You can do the same. If you don't travel often, or this seems like a stretch, begin with something small. Maybe you enjoy going to Starbucks (or whatever your favorite coffee shop might be). Every time you go, expect something nice to happen there. Even if it doesn't happen, keep expecting it. It could begin with a really kind word from the Barista that makes your day brighter.

Or maybe they "mess up" your drink so you receive a free one next time. Perhaps you are in the drive through at Starbucks and the person in front of you pays for your drink. Starbucks miracles happen consistently for my husband because he just knows he's going to get them! He's received Starbucks gifts cards, free drink cards, and he's had other people pay for his drinks. Those experiences strengthen his beliefs and expectations about the miracles that are possible in other areas of his life, and he applies them there. (He's had so many miracles happen in his professional career that I've lost count!)

Of course as I was editing this chapter, Bobbi Li, my favorite Caribou Barista, gifted me a free cup of coffee. Confirmation!

WHAT DO YOU EXPECT?

Now it's time to dig into YOUR expectations. What do you expect to show up in your personal and professional life? Unfortunately, I'm not talking about the good stuff here. I'm talking about the things that you don't want. For example, perhaps you just expect to "get by" every month but not actually make a dent in your debt because "there's just never enough money." So, do you get what you expect?

I want you to take a moment and actually write down all of the negative things you expect to just happen every month. You might not have thought about your expectations in this way in the past, but I want you to see that this is always working for you, just perhaps not the way you want it to. The good news is that you can absolutely change your expectations to what you really want, but you have to become clear on where you are right now with this. For example, maybe you expect to only make

$4,000 each month, but it's not enough to pay the bills. Perhaps you expect to feel super stressed out at the end of every month because there's not enough money to take care of your family.

What are the top three (negative) things that you expect to happen every month?

1. _____

2. _____

3. _____

An easy way to figure out what you'd like to expect, is to simply flip these items into positive expectations. They are usually the opposite of what you don't what. For example, you really want to make $6,000 or more per month so you can pay all of your bills, save for retirement, tithe, and have enough money to pay down your student loan.

What are the top three (positive) things that you'd like to expect to happen every month?

1. _____

2. _____

3. _____

Now that's all well and good, except I want you to dream bigger and ask for even more. Dig deep and go to the next level. Ask yourself, "What do I REALLY wish I expected to happen every month?" For example, perhaps you really wish that you could expect to make $10,000 or more per month so you can pay all of your bills, save for retirement, tithe, put money away for vacations, save for your child's college education, and have enough money to pay down your student loan.

Do you see the difference? Getting clear on what you truly want to expect can help take your One Great Goal to an entirely new level!

Let's do this one more time.

What are the top three (positive) things that you'd *REALLY* like to expect to happen every month?

1. _____

2. _____

3. _____

Good! Now you are finally ready to receive those great things.

FROM EXPECTATION TO KNOWING

I remember when I was struggling with writing this book and how I wanted to proceed. I had so many Limiting Beliefs coming up about why I shouldn't write it, that it was too "out there," that it took away from my main expertise in sales. My inner critic was just having a field day!

And so I did what I know how to do. I shifted beliefs as they came up, and I prayed. I asked God to show me a sign that I was on the right path. That I really should write this book. That it was meant to be out in the world. And then I forgot my prayer until an amazing miracle shifted me from EXPECTING to KNOWING that I was supposed to write this book because of the millions of people it will help.

I'm a big fan of Joel Osteen. Some labeled him a "Prosperity Preacher" (as if there's something inherently wrong with prosperity?) and I LOVE THAT! Joel's message is that it's okay to be close to God while living a prosperous life. In fact, it's pretty tough to make the impact we want to make without being prosperous.

I can remember watching him on television when we were in the middle of the Great Recession. It was his voice that often lifted me up when I was having some of my toughest days. It was his voice and his books that reminded me I can transform any situation simply by saying "I Am" and then filling in the blank. (By the way, I love his inspirational book, *The Power of I Am*.)

And so I started to say, "I AM going to write that book. It IS going to be a bestseller. I AM going to impact millions of people."

I wrote it down. I said it to myself. And I silenced the inner critic that was trying so hard to shut me down.

My sign hadn't shown up yet, but I didn't give up hope. I just kept asking and expecting.

One day I came across a pen from the Montage Hotel in Laguna Beach, California. A pen doesn't seem like a big deal, but when I picked it up, a tingle ran up and down my spine. It felt like some sort of sign. It was a particularly gorgeous white pen with gold writing on it, and I heard this voice in my head, *"Go to the Montage."*

That evening, I was driving to another appointment and I looked up and to the right just in time to see the sign for the Montage—I was driving past it!

"Strange," I whispered to myself.

I didn't realize it was so close to where I've been working.

The next day, before I left California, one of my clients said, "If you ever want to go somewhere amazing to be inspired, go to the Montage Hotel and have a glass of wine on their patio which overlooks the Pacific Ocean."

Really? Did I hear her correctly?

I called up one of my dear friends and asked her to go to dinner with me that night—at the Montage. She already had plans (a Divine "block" so to speak), so I decided not to go that night and instead got on a plane back to Minneapolis, vowing to make it back.

I made a commitment to go there the next time I was in town, which was a week later. I was speaking at an event in Capistrano Beach, and my dear friend happened to be at the event.

"Let's go to the Montage for dinner after this. I keep getting signs I am supposed to go there."

She's used to me saying things like that and living in the magic, so she just nodded "Yes" and said, "It sounds great to me!"

If you haven't been there, the Montage IS an exquisite hotel with a gorgeous patio to enjoy a glass of wine. We sat out on the patio drinking wine all alone (we felt like VIP's) because it was a quiet Wednesday evening.

There was a cool breeze coming in from the Pacific Ocean, so our server moved a heater closer and gave us each a blanket (yes, a soft blanket) to keep us warm. The wind picked up and suddenly it started to rain, so our server moved us inside before serving us dinner. As he was relocating us, I looked up and saw another server ushering in a party of three from the other patio.

No, it can't be.

But there he was. Joel Osteen and his beautiful wife, Victoria, were also getting out of the rain. They were ushered to a private table on the other side of the restaurant.

After we were seated, I looked at my friend and I said, "That's it! That's the sign! Joel was my reminder to BELIEVE in the book I AM writing and to keep going."

She smiled at me and exclaimed, "Of course!"

By the time Joel and his wife left the restaurant, which had become quite crowded. But before he walked out the door, he turned to my friend and me, nodded and smiled. I am telling you, we were the only two people that he greeted in that restaurant.

I am so grateful to the Universe for guiding me to that moment, that reminder, and to Joel Osteen for reminding me of the power of I AM.

That experienced shifted me from expecting that this book was going to be written and change lives to KNOWING it will.

Your sign is waiting for you, too. Just watch!

QUANTUM CORNER

ANDREA GRIBBLE

#SocialSchool4EDU

www.SocialSchool4EDU.com

AFTER SALES CAMP, I tripled my sales. I went from $40K in revenue to $120K. And then after being part of the Synchronize program, I doubled my sales from $120K to $240K. The area where I needed the most clarity was realizing that I was adding value to the schools I serve and I was not bothering them when I reached out. I also had this belief that they didn't have money for my service.

My biggest discovery at Sales Camp was that I was trying to do too much! Things would fall in line if I just focused on getting more social media customers. I was trying to sell a book. I was trying to book speaking gigs. Everything would fall in line if I could just get to 12 schools!

The habits and practices that helped me reach my goals the most are that I wake up everyday with an attitude of gratitude—so thankful that I get to have the best "job" in the world. I'm also very focused on bringing on more stay-at-home Moms onto my team. That passion to provide them with an opportunity to earn income while being a great parent drives me to make those phone calls, do the follow-ups, and create the momentum required to provide that.

Before Sales Camp, I thought selling was hard and that I was bothering people. Before Sales Camp, I actually thought I was pretty good when I could actually book the appointment— but getting the appointment was the tough part. I just didn't have a system to generate consistent appointments. At Sales Camp, I created a new belief, "Money flows easily to my family because I help schools and solve their SM problems." That new belief helped me gain confidence and I started to set intentions before I made the phone calls.

The three actions that helped me double and triple my sales were consistent calls, tracking my numbers, and focused effort toward my One Great Goal.

Since Sales Camp and Synchronize, I now KNOW that selling is easy because I add extreme value for my schools. I also KNOW that I know that I have a million-dollar business (and beyond). I know that my business model is sound. I believe that great things are about to happen—every day!

Step #7: Create

"Because you have so little faith. Truly I tell you, if you have faith as small as a mustard seed, you can say to this mountain, 'Move from here to there,' and it will move. Nothing will be impossible for you."

~ Matthew 17:20 | NIV ~

AFTER A YEAR of amazing opportunity and growth as a family and in my business, Tim and I got very clear that the next step for us was finding a Lake House and creating the vision we had held in our hearts for many years. Now, this may not seem like a really big deal, but remember what I shared with you about our previous experience in real estate—the crash and all of the losses? It was a big deal for us to have dug ourselves out of that and to be willing to dive back into real estate again. And, of course, the houses we really loved around the lake were going for half a million dollars and more.

We were clear about exactly what we wanted and clear about how much we wanted to spend (not a half a million dollars) on a house that we could renovate into our dream house.

As with all of my goals, I started writing this one down on my goal list—with a checkbox next to it, of course! I started to sync up with the vibration of the Lake House, using my imagination to experience what it felt like to live in the Lake House. We even picked out a house on the lake that we just loved. I drove past it almost every day and imagined what it would be like to live in that house on that lake. I took a picture of it on my iPhone and looked at it daily.

Of course, Tim and I both had to shift some of our Limiting Beliefs and release some fears after our previous experiences. But we knew how to do that and navigated the journey well together, reminding ourselves and each other that we had learned a lot and were wiser and ready for this new adventure.

The day we stepped into THE Lake House for the first time, we knew it was the one. And, guess what? It was just a block away from the house that we had fallen in love with and very similar. It's a split-level, so we walked straight up the stairs into the living room and looked straight out to the lake. There was something so unique and magical about this property, even more than we had hoped for. The moment we saw that view, we both looked at each other and said, barely breathing, "That's a million-dollar view." We also were thrilled that it wasn't going to cost us a million dollars, or even half a million. We calculated renovations and decided that this was the right place for us. In that moment, we decided.

"The first offer on the house fell through, so they took it off the market for a bit," the realtor broke into our moment. "They just put it back on and they already have an offer, but they haven't accepted it yet."

"Well," Tim responded, "we'd like to put an offer in as well. The house needs some work, so we're going to offer a little less than asking price, but we're ready."

And then we went home and panicked! What if they didn't accept our offer? What if they did? Were we up for the work? Would our current home sell fast enough?

We agreed to stop the panic and step into the New Belief Zone of possibility, gratitude, and peace... and let it be.

They accepted our offer immediately, and our home sold in eight days. Yes, eight days!

We created the reality of owning a beautiful Lake House!

And guess what? I'm finishing this last chapter of the book looking at the million-dollar view, while the renovations are going on seamlessly.

This Belief Zone stuff works—I'm telling you!

And Creating is the last step in the process.

YOU ARE A POWERFUL CREATOR

By now, you have read the word "create" or "creation" in this book almost one hundred times. Why? Because I wanted this book to reveal to you that you are not a victim of your situation. You are a powerful creator who now has the skills and the knowledge you need to create the income and life you desire.

This chapter was originally about receiving, because I'd been taught that receiving was the final step in creation for so long. And then, after more reading and studying of Quantum Physics, it became very clear to me that it has never been about receiving, because receiving means that I have to wait for something whereas creating means I bring it into reality myself. Internal vs. External. Victim vs. Creator. I want you to know, in the deepest part of you, that you have never been a victim of your circumstances. You are not sentenced to only "having so much" in life because of who you are, how you were raised, or where you came from. You are a child of God who can create anything that you dream. And, this is your moment. Will you take it?

Like most new mothers, I will never forget the first time I held my child in my arms. Yes, it was a powerful moment. It was also the moment when I deeply understood the power of creation. Nine months before, he was just a dream. And then, here he was in our physical reality.

I thought I was a terrible creator most of my life. I didn't believe that I deserved things or that I had the power to create something different in my life. My childhood was "interesting" at times and my ability and belief in myself to create what I desired broke at some point. Someone once said to me, "When you were young, you put the best parts of you into a secret place, and as you got older, you slowly started to let them out because it was safe."

Part of "letting them out" meant being my truest, most authentic self and no longer caring what people thought about me (or, caring less... and not letting it stop me). That wasn't easy.

The big question that loomed when I finally learned how to create what I really wanted vs. what I didn't want had to do with taking the brakes off. One of my coaches asked me, "How much success are you willing to allow yourself to have?"

The question by itself assumes that success is external—that I can only allow a certain about of success in. But my study of

Quantum Physics and the Belief Zone have revealed that th question was, "How much success am I willing to create?"

And that is the same question you should be asking yourself right now.

How much success are you willing to create right now in your life?

THE LAW OF POLARITY

One of the key lessons that I learned about creating was that in order to create *more*, you had to be willing to create *everything*. One more time, because that concept is where all of the gold of this step is. In order to create *anything*, you had to be willing to create *everything*.

I don't remember where I heard it for the first time, but then it started to show up everywhere, so I knew it was something that I needed to learn. In order to take the brakes off, in order to create what I really wanted, I had to be willing to create the bad and the ugly along with the good. And for the longest time, I hadn't been willing to allow the ugly.

I didn't want the criticism that might come from creating more visibility.

I didn't want the bad book reviews that might come with the good ones.

I didn't want the few client complaints that might come in addition to the hundreds and hundreds of happy clients that had shown up.

And then one day, I got tired of resisting what I perceived as the "bad." I got tired of keeping the brakes on. And I decided that it was time to really build my creative muscle.

I changed my programs. I doubled what I was charging. I said NO to more things. I started flying first class whenever I could. I stayed in the nicest hotels. (Okay, well, nicer hotels and sometimes the nicest! I'm still kind of frugal!) I stopped caring so much about what people thought. And because of that, I was able to serve my clients even more and create the best year ever both personally and professionally.

And then I had one of the most major "aha" moments of my life. I realized that if I could create what I really wanted, my desires, I didn't HAVE to create the "bad" (or what I perceived as "bad") with it. I could just create my desires.

Thank you, Lucca, for getting the ball rolling with that lesson.

And I'm so glad we moved back to Minnesota.

THE ENERGY OF CREATING

Once you have completed the "hard work" of getting clear on what you want, releasing Limiting Beliefs, and changing your expectations, then it's time to commit to creating your greatest desires.

At one point in your life, you were probably a really good creator. As very young children, we love to create! I remember, as a child, thinking that I could draw anything. And I could! Was it always perfect? No. But I believed I could draw and create in that way and my drawing improved as I got older.

Unfortunately, as we get older, society begins to teach us to compare ourselves to others. We are told what talent is. We are told what intelligence is. We are told how to act at all times. And when we feel like we don't measure up in a certain area, we stop trying. We stop creating. And we begin to believe all of the lies around us about not being good enough or smart enough, and then we begin to settle for mediocrity—because we don't believe that we can create what WE want. Through elementary and high school, we continue to be told that it is "best to only focus on what we can make a good living at." Some of us are almost shamed for venturing out and trying a career path that is unconventional. We are taught that the world is unpredictable and scary. We are conditioned to stay in our Comfort Zone and take the safest path possible that leads to a predictable living, even if it's a life we didn't desire to create.

And then we wonder why we aren't good at creating money—or anything—when we become adults.

And then we perpetuate the cycle with our kids. Why would we ever tell them that they can create when we don't believe we can?

And then they end up "broken creators," like us.

There's a scene from the movie Office Space where one of the characters, Milton, is notorious for being the first person in line when someone in the office has a birthday. In one scene, he is told to move to the back of the line. And so he does, and by the time he gets to the front of the line, there isn't any cake left.

For so many people, this is their truth. We've been brainwashed to think that only by waiting for the right time, the right next step, etc., will we create the life and income that we desire. But that's not the truth. You have step up and claim the piece of cake that is yours. You do that by taking the steps I've outlined in this book, and then you take the final step of creating and bring your desire into reality.

Let me be clear, I love to give. My mission is to help entrepreneurs and sales professionals make a lot of money so they can give back to the organizations they care about—AND live a great life. I want to impact millions with my message. What is the impact that you want to make? Too often I find that people have given, and given, and given and they haven't taken the time to create great clients, opportunities, money, health, love, etc. for themselves. How could they? They've been too busy giving, thinking that is the path to their success.

Ladies, this is especially true for us.

Think about it! If you knew without a doubt that you were an awesome creator (which you are), what would you do differently in your life? In your business?

You would create great clients.

You would create great gifts.

You would create a lot of money.

You would create a life where everything goes well for you.

And it will.

THE FREQUENCY OF CREATING

One of my clients thought about joining our Synchronize Coaching program for about six months after she took Sales Camp. She kept saying she wanted to be in the program but didn't make the commitment. I didn't try to convince her because I knew she already had a deep desire to join the program, but it had to be her decision. I released her. And then she saw me speak again and walked up immediately afterward and said, "I am hiring you. I don't even care how much it costs. I know you've doubled your prices again and I know it's worth it."

In that moment, she and I BOTH had to be ready to create. I had to be willing to honor her and not say, "Oh, that's okay, you can have the price of the old program." No, she wanted the new program because she KNEW it would help HER create the goals that she desired. And, I needed to stand in my New Belief Zone, which included my new frequency. She wanted to invest in herself at the higher price point because she knew she was worth it (her frequency was higher). And so I said yes, and I created a new client.

A week after our FIRST coaching session, after she had doubled the prices in her program (think thousands of dollars, not hundreds!), and someone from her top 20% immediately hired her and was thrilled to do so. She had created that client with glee. When I spoke with her during her next session, she told me she was thrilled by what was happening.

I asked her, "What do you believe now about sales and money?"

She answered, "It's even more than a belief. I KNOW I can reach my sales goals now. In fact, I am setting new goals as we speak because I know I am going to surpass them. But it's more than that. I can feel it in my body. Something has shifted. I feel different. I think different. I am different."

The frequency of creating is light. It's joyful. It's more about being the happiest version of you that knows and trusts that you can create anything you want in your life. It's about moving from fear to fierce, and being on the leading edge of creation every single day.

As I sit here, looking at the lake right outside my home office window, I am KNOWING that it's time for YOU to dream big again and create all your heart desires—professionally and personally.

And I can't wait to hear all about it!

QUANTUM CORNER

ABIGAIL WALKER

Vivian Lou

www.vivianlou.com

I FIRST MET URSULA at a free 2-hour seminar for entrepreneurs. After listening to her amazing presentation, I felt compelled to ask her opinion about my product and pricing. I stayed after the presentation and told her about my product. Without even seeing or trying the product, she asked me if I thought it was priced appropriately. I said no and that I should be charging more. She confirmed. And told me I needed to at least double my price (i.e. 1 insole for $19.95). She was so matter of fact and so unapologetic about her statement. After seeing my shock, she looked at me again and said, "Do it tomorrow." I was incredibly excited and nervous that she was so confident in this plan without knowing my product or me. And I thought... *Why not?* So I did. The very next day. I was so nervous about people hating the product and me. I received a total of 2 unhappy emails. Not bad! Now I KNOW that you have to charge what you're worth.

Before Sales Camp, I believed that I couldn't make the "ask." I literally had a physical resistance (couldn't write, sweaty palms, sick to my stomach) about asking for a sale. And I didn't even sell in-person. These were the reactions I would get sending a weekly email to my email list. J I also had some pretty Limiting Beliefs. I didn't believe I was qualified or worthy, that I didn't have the experience, and that I couldn't see myself making "big" money. I also didn't know where to go first—doctor offices, retail, ecommerce, etc.

In June 2015, I went through Sales Camp for the first time. During Sales Camp, you have to outline and call your ideal clients. I debated whether to approach smaller boutiques and chiropractor's offices or MY DREAM retail partner—Nordstrom. I spent way too long hemming and hawing and Ursula simply asked, "Why play small?" Point taken. I called up Nordstrom and was connected with the buyer for high heel insoles. (The product isn't in Nordstrom yet...but it will be.) I then discovered that I needed to dream even bigger!

In the past, I was always so ashamed of saying that I was in business to make money. What I discovered during the One Great Goal exercise is that my goal is to make money. Period. And I am no longer ashamed to admit it. I'm not out to make money just to be 'rich' or acquire expensive items. I want to make money so that my husband can retire from his corporate job and manage properties (his lifelong dream!). I want to make money so that my kids can go to college debt-free. I want to make money so that my husband and I can travel the world with our kiddos. I want to make money so that I can acquire experiences...and I am FINALLY okay with saying that. J

The second time I did Sales Camp, I wanted feedback on how to expand my business. Ursula encouraged me to pick up the phone and call CEO of HSN and CEO of STORY to ask their advice. Both returned my calls promptly and were willing to help. My clarity came from moving and taking action. Picking up the phone. Sending an email. Making a decision. Ironically, I learned that I didn't want to be in retail and that I wasn't ready to expand my product line. Both HUGE moments of clarity. In a roundabout way, I confirmed what my gut was telling me—focus on ecommerce and ecommerce alone. Perhaps the biggest benefit of Sales Camp was being in a room full of people who believed in me. It was the first time I had really been fully immersed in a learning environment with other entrepreneurs. That energy, being channeled and focused and led by such an inspirational woman, was unlike anything I'd ever experienced or have yet to experience again!

In late April 2016, I attended Sales Camp again. I had just sold out on HSN 3 times, but I was still doing roughly on $2k-$3k/month in sales. It was an extremely emotional experience as I knew there was so much potential for this business, but I wasn't getting there or at least as fast as I wanted. I was surrounded by all of these other really motivated folks—mostly women—who were so encouraging and truly believed that I would make it! So I signed up for SYNCHRONIZE and literally started crying as I knew it would be life-changing. My first two meetings with Ursula were so refreshing. She kept reminding me how far I had come in such a short amount of time and reassured me that the money will come. She also kept reminding me that I had this ability to make decisions quickly, implement, and manifest.

The #1 habit I shifted is I've learned to love the numbers. That's easy to say when you're making money, but Ursula pushed me to put together a mock forecast. It was VERY painful, but I realized that the potential to make money was not as difficult as I was imagining. I now LOVE looking at the numbers. I track spend, revenue, and ROI every single day. It's fascinating.

I've also learned to dream big. Who the HELL would have thought that a girl who couldn't even talk about $10,000 a month less than 2 years ago is now forecasting to make $500,000 a month at the end of 2017? Once I got over the hurdle and shame and resistance to talking about and thinking about money, it started to flow.

I've learned SO much through the Sales Camp/Synchronize process. I cannot tell you how freeing, how exhilarating, how fun it is to live in this New Belief Zone. I trust the Universe so much more (and thank IT everyday for not giving up on me when I thought I had to control everything). I trust myself so much more. I know I will make mistakes, but the most important thing is to keep moving.

Things happen so quickly for me... and I've learned to trust it. Enjoy the ride. Learn. Make decisions. Fail quickly and recover. Keep moving. It's because of these new beliefs that I know I won't fail. Businesses may fail, but I won't. Beyoncé once said, "I don't like to gamble, but if there's one thing I'm willing to bet on, it's myself." When I first read her quote, I was stunned. I wanted to believe in myself the way she did. And today, I do. It is an awesome feeling to be willing and able to take the bet on myself.

The three actions that made the biggest impact on my sales growth were raising my prices, refusing to continue being intimidated, and starting to believe in myself.

You have to claim what you want. My time with Ursula and Rebekah during Synchronize was much more about that than it was about the numbers. When I first started, I was embarrassed to say out loud how much I wanted to make. I was scared. I was ashamed. I was timid. I quickly learned that it's not only okay, but necessary, to state what you want. The more I said it, the more I believed it would happen... and it has ...faster and more fruitfully than I actually imagined!!

Plus, don't be intimidated. In the summer of 2016, I had a not-so-ideal interaction with HSN. While being associated with the program is great and has led to many opportunities, Rebekah frequently reminded me that I don't have to be bullied by the big guys or intimidated by the numbers. She reminded me about the runway with ecommerce and the challenges with wholesale. I loved her advice regarding always "being grateful for the opportunity, but you don't have to stay in any arrangement that isn't beneficial to you or the bottom line. Just remember to exit with grace."

I started Sales Camp (the first time) making $1500/month. The second time, I was making $3000/mo. I have since 100x the size of my business and have set a goal to 6x the size of my business this year.

And now I KNOW that I write my own story. There have been several times when Ursula has reminded me that I have a pretty crazy story and one that changes almost weekly. She encourages me to keep notes because one day, I will present my story and or write a book.

As a result of Sales Camp and Synchronize, I believe in myself more than I ever have—and that is an unbelievable gift!

THE BELIEF ZONE
BLUEPRINT

"Don't be afraid of what others think of you.
Be afraid of who you will become if you continue to care."

~ Ursula Mentjes ~

Now THAT YOU understand the power and importance of your Belief Zone, it's time to explain The Belief Zone Blueprint so that you can create a BZB (Belief Zone Blueprint) for yourself and fast-track yourself through the process.

Let's take a moment to understand what a blueprint is. Random House Dictionary tells us that a blueprint is *"a detailed outline, a plan of action."* The Belief Zone Blueprint is your unique plan of action that allows you to not only get into The Belief Zone, but stay there, and achieve the goals you've set for yourself.

When I first thought about The Belief Zone Blueprint, it reminded me of a fingerprint. Just like a fingerprint, no Belief Zone Blueprint will be exactly the same because everyone is different. Every Limiting Belief is going to be slightly different. Every new Achieving Belief is going to be different. Every challenge to reach your goals will be different. So each Belief Zone Blueprint must be different.

That's what I love about the coaching work I do with my clients. Every breakthrough that my clients experience is different because what it took to reach their breakdown is unique to their experience and so the new experience that they decide to create will be uniquely different. Plus, the breakthroughs come much faster when I hold the new belief with my client—before it can catch up and become a part of their New Belief Zone Blueprint. By holding that belief with them, they can begin to take actions outside of their Comfort Zone because I am essentially giving them the confidence to move forward in spite of their Limiting Beliefs.

Creating your own Belief Zone Blueprint happens by simply following the steps that I've already outlined in the book for you along with some additional suggestions to keep you in it.

Your Belief Zone Blueprint

Now that you understand the power and importance of The Belief Zone Blueprint, it's time to create your own.

The process of creating your own Belief Zone Blueprint will help you do three things: clarify what you want, identify the negative beliefs attached to each goal that might stop you from achieving your goals, and then move you into a new frequency to help you stay in The Belief Zone.

Grab your favorite journal again and get ready to write!

STEP #1: CLARIFY

Review your top 50 goals and your One Great Goal. This is your opportunity to review those goals and take yourself through the OGG process once again. Then, write your goal list down along with your One Great Goal. Are you committed to this list? Is it in total alignment with you? Do a triple check.

_____

_____

_____

STEP #2: WRITE

Next, it's time to write your fifty goals as if they are part of a checklist—as if you BELIEVE 100% (because you do!) that those goals are on their way into reality. Write your checklist now and as you write it, feel those feelings of expectation and what it will be like once you've achieved those goals. Be sure to include your new monthly and annual Sales Goal.

Your One Great Goal:

Monthly and Annual Sales Goal:

Goal #1:

Goal #2:

Goal #3:

Goal #4:

Goal #5:

Then, date a journal entry in the future (less than a year, more than a week) and detail out exactly how your goals came to life. Remember to write in the present tense as if it has already happened.

STEP #3: SYNC

Remember, this is the part where you get to release your goals on faith so you can raise your frequency—letting go of having to focus on it 24-7, giving it up to God or however you want to say it, *still believing* that it will happen. You let go of your fear that it won't happen. When you release fear, only full faith, anticipation, and expectation are left. What do you need to let go of so you can move forward in full faith that your goals on are their way to you?

STEP #4: SHIFT

Remember, this is your chance to blast through and shift those Limiting Beliefs so you can move into a New Belief Zone. Again, a quick way to discover your Limiting Beliefs is to ask yourself, "What do I believe about achieving my One Great Goal and the other goals on my list?" That usually brings up your Limiting Beliefs pretty quickly so you can address them and take yourself through the belief change process. Here is a quick version of that process so you can take yourself through it any time. I recommend using this version after you've mastered the version earlier in the book.

1. Write down your Limiting Belief:

---

2. What are three things that aren't true about that Limiting Belief?

_____

_____

_____

3. What is the Achieving Belief you want to put in its place?

_____

_____

_____

4. If you took on this the belief, what different actions would you take?

_____

_____

_____

5. If you took on this new belief, how would you "show up" differently?

_____

_____

_____

Then, commit to taking the new actions that you wrote down above. And, no matter what, keep going. It takes time for a new belief to develop into a permanent belief.

Step #5: Act

Remember, you have to get all in. You can't be 50% in to your goals. You have to actually decide that this is what you want. You have to commit. You KNOW you are 100% committed when you no longer have a backup plan. And once you are all in, the action steps show up. You might not want to take them because they are outside of your Comfort Zone, but those are the exact steps that will get you there—and that's how you will know that they are the right steps. What are the first 2-5 steps that you can see in front of you right now? Write them down and write a completion date next to them.

_____

_____

_____

Step #6: Know

You're clear, you've made a decision, you've written your list of goals, you've released fear and shifted Limiting Beliefs, so now it's time to move into expectation. Expectation is a feeling of knowing and trusting that your goal is on the way. If you don't feel that way, then it's important to go back through the Limiting Belief process to see what might be getting in your way.

What does it feel like to expect that your goal is on its way to you?

_____

_____

_____

STEP #7: CREATE

Oh, yes, the art of creating! You've done all of the "hard" work, now it's time to bring your goals into reality! This is the exact place that you MUST push through and continue to manage your thoughts, beliefs, and expectations (your frequency) so you can more easily create the goals that are coming into your reality! Do not let your Limiting Beliefs stop the goals and financial prosperity from showing up. Again, Limiting Beliefs can pop up any time, so if you get all the way to step seven and you suddenly find yourself unable to create small gifts, compliments, money, etc., then go back up to Step #3 or Step #4 and figure out what you need to let go of so you can easily create your desires.

Are you truly ready to create? How do you know? What has shifted?

_____

_____

_____

Conclusion: Persevere

"When you get into a tight place and everything goes against you ... never give up then, for that is just the place and time that the tide will turn."

~ Harriet Beecher Stowe ~

IN THE BEGINNING of this journey, what's most important is that you *discern the difference* between your Comfort Zone and your New Belief Zone. The easiest way to master discernment is to notice how you feel.

When you are out of your chosen Belief Zone, you are in your "old" belief zone—your Comfort Zone—where things just don't seem to go the way you hoped. Murphy's Law will seemingly rule the day and everything might seem to go wrong. In the area of your finances, it's as if you can't win and bill after bill just seems to pile up. Money seems to be "stuck" and not flowing to you. Sales stop coming in. Life just seems like it has slowed down and you probably feel frustrated, angry, and stuck.

When you are in your New Belief Zone, you will experience more ease and flow and synchronicity. The right people and situations will appear in your life, and you will achieve your goals quickly and easily.

Many authors and self-help gurus have talked about this. Joseph Campbell was one of the first to say, "Follow your bliss." He was talking directly about how you feel. If you feel blissful, you will be in a powerful frequency, which will allow positive things to be attracted to you. If you are in a primarily negative state (having negative thoughts), you will attract negative opportunities to you because of the frequency you are in. By following your bliss and feeling great no matter what, you will stay in a positive state. The goal is to lean more toward the positive state than the negative state. I like to "watch" my thoughts pass by in my head and, rather than emotionally attaching to the negative thoughts, to simply observe them and say, "Isn't that interesting?"

There will be serious events that happen in life, though, that might not allow you to feel blissful. The loss of a loved one will impact feelings of bliss for sure. It's important to remember that you can still manage those feelings of loss so that you don't dip into a deep depression or spiral downward even more. And the truth is, the person you lost wouldn't want you to be depressed either; they would want you to find your bliss again.

As I mentioned earlier, Abraham and Esther Hicks talk about following your most joyful feelings in their bestselling series of books. Specifically, they talk about staying in the flow by having you imagine that you are floating down a river. When your feelings are in a negative state, it's almost like you are attempting to paddle your canoe upstream versus just flowing downstream. When you are in a more positive state, you will begin to flow down the river more easily, or just go with the flow. When you are really going with the flow, you will begin to move even faster down that river and you will notice that sales, money, and other things you want are flowing to you very easily.

They advise you to keep track of your feelings and measure their intensity. Imagine that feelings run on a continuum from very sad and dark to extremely positive all the way to bliss, joy, and love. It might be difficult to jump from very sad to bliss, but you might be able to move from very sad to less sad, to happy, and then on to bliss—or something like that. In other words, become aware of your feelings and begin to manage them throughout your days. You will find that over time you will begin to move more quickly from a negative state to a positive state much faster.

As an NLP certified coach, I have learned the power of state changes and moving my clients from negative states to positive states. One way that NLP teaches you to make a quick state change (if you are in a negative state) is to imagine a time when something really positive happened to you. Imagine that moment in your mind and add color, sound, and feeling to that moment. When you connect all of your senses to that moment in time, along with how you felt, you will automatically shift your state. The more you shift into that state, the more you will begin to reside there. It's like building any other muscle.

This is a great way to practice continual state changes so you will truly be able to find, and follow, your bliss after you've taken yourself through the Belief Zone Blueprint. Your bliss is what will allow your goals to easily manifest in a "great feeling" space.

Richard Dotts, in his book, *Thoughtless Magic*, talks about the power of being in a *thoughtless* state. He says that by choosing an intention without words, you simply create the feeling of the completed intention! Brilliant! This feeling, again, is what can catapult you—and keep you—in The Belief Zone.

I hope you are beginning to see how powerful your New Belief Zone really can be. I spend most of my days now in my New Belief Zone—the one that I've chosen, the one that I created, the one that holds infinite possibility. And what I want you to see is that it is available for you, too.

You are also most likely beginning to formulate a question like this one: "Once I am in a New Belief Zone, how do I stay in it?"

What Happens if I Fall Out?

One of the tools that I created for my clients was a Crisis Tool Kit to support them when they "fall out." I have included 10 basic steps that will help you stop the downward spiral so you can reengage and get refocused.

As you engage in stepping into The Belief Zone, there may be times where "obstacles" show up. I put obstacles in quotes because they aren't really obstacles. Often they are gifts that have shown up to either stretch you (to release an old belief and create a new one) or to help you move past old emotions or experiences. It doesn't really matter why they showed up; this is your opportunity to release them.

The 10 steps below are designed to pull you out of a downward (negative) emotional spin and move you into a positive upward spin—back to focusing on what you desire to create, rather than on what you don't want. Use this process whenever you begin to spiral downward.

THE 10 STEPS TO STOP THE SPIRAL:

1) Acknowledge the challenge, negative emotion or issue at hand.

2) Feel the emotion (or the emotion tied to the challenge or issue at hand) in full. Expand it to a level 10 and just acknowledge what's there.

3) Write down the emotion that's showing up. Is it fear? Anger? What's underneath the emotion?

4) And then, ask yourself, "What's not true about this emotion as it's tied to this situation?" Write down everything that shows up for you that's not true about.

5) Take 10 deep breaths, slowly in and slowly out, fully feeling the emotion to a level 10—until it almost feels as if it POPS! Once it has released, take 10 more deep breaths, slowly in and out. Continue to relax and as you breathe in and out slowly, allow the final bits of emotion to completely release.

6) Then, think of a time when you felt extremely successful. Access that state. Imagine that you are there, in the moment, fully feeling it. Engage your senses. What do you see? Notice the faces—who is there with you? (Enhance the colors around.) Notice the sounds you hear? What are the scents that you smell? Most importantly, what does it feel like in your core area (stomach/gut) to achieve this goal? In your "mind's eye," fully step into that moment in time.

7) Notice this feeling—is it a feeling of success? Peace? Confidence? Recognize that when you focus on the new feeling, that old feeling dissolves. Allow that feeling to expand to a level 10!

8) As soon as you have fully accessed this feeling, put your right hand on your heart to anchor this feeling. Anchoring is an NLP (Neuro-Linguistic Programming) term and it simply means that you will be able to recall this feeling whenever you need it.

9) Continue to place your right hand on your heart throughout the day to access that feeling of confidence, peace, success—of whatever that is for you. Do this for a full five minutes. Enjoy this feeling!

10) In the future, when you begin to spiral downward, put your hand on your heart to immediately come back to this feeling of success. Or, take yourself through the steps again if you cannot shake it.

The truth is, you WILL fall out. But as long as you get back up and keep going, nothing will stop you.

Eleanor Roosevelt once said, "You must do that thing you think you cannot do." It's time. Don't let this opportunity pass to get out of your Comfort Zone and into the best Belief Zone your imagination can conjure.

PERSEVERE

If there is anything I have learned through my entrepreneurial journey, it's that you never actually "arrive" anywhere. It's a constant unfolding of the "next." There are many, many, many things that I have not wanted to do in my business because they were way outside of my Comfort Zone. But, I persevered, did it anyway, and incredible results and next steps were always on the other side.

Random House Dictionary reminds us that to persevere means, *"to persist in anything undertaken; maintain a purpose in spite of difficulty, obstacles, or discouragement; continue steadfastly."* You are going to come up against situations, obstacles, disappointments, discouragement, and things that are just uncomfortable. But take the time to discern the difference between being uncomfortable and something not being a good fit. By doing this, you will always be pushing the edge of your Belief Zone.

Most people don't know it, but I am actually an introvert. Maybe an ambivert (which is a little bit of both introvert and extrovert). Being a professional speaker was WAY outside of my Comfort Zone in the beginning of my career. But I worked on my speaking skills for years. I actually got better over time, through a lot of practice, and now people have a hard time believing that I am a recovering introvert!

And then, it happened—the next big leap out of my Comfort Zone. My team asked me to deliver a training on Facebook Live. The old fears and Limiting Beliefs came back up. Even as a recovering introvert, putting myself out on Facebook, or any Social Media, has been difficult. I'm the person who edits my posts ten times before hitting the post button! But, since Facebook Live was the next thing I was afraid to do, I knew it was the exact thing I needed to do that would move me into the my next New Belief Zone. My first Facebook Live post had almost 3,000 views! I was shocked. My team was shocked. As my New Belief Zone expanded regarding how I could grow my platform, so did my capacity to deliver, and so will yours.

It's always sad for me to end a book because I feel like we've been on a special journey together. I don't want to lose you. I don't want you to lose your path. Yes, I am speaking directly to you. If you haven't yet, go back and take yourself through all of the exercises in this book. Commit to the process as you move into a New Belief Zone and then make a decision to stay there until you expand into your next New Belief Zone.

You know what to do.

A Special Invitation from Ursula

FREE gift from Ursula!

Every wonder what the **Top 10%** of Sales Pros and Entrepreneurs do to be successful every day?

Then take this special opportunity to find out! Ursula has developed a Mini Video Course just for you to find out the *Sales Secrets of the Top 10%*! Just go to <u>www.SalesCoachNow.com</u> to register for this course. Again, it's a $497 value but you can get it for **FREE!**

For Non-Profits

Our Mission is to help entrepreneurs and sales professionals make a lot of money so they can live a rewarding life AND give back to the nonprofit organizations they care about. To help reach that goal, we have launched our new Profit Forward program, designed to connect nonprofits with for profit organizations AND give them the sales training they need to increase their funding.

If you are the Executive Director, Founder, or Fundraising Professional for a nonprofit, and this is your sole focus, then we invite you to apply for a full scholarship to attend: http://www.salescoachnow.com/for-non-profits/

THE DOUBLE YOUR SALES NOW PODCAST

Join Ursula on the Double Your Sales NOW Podcast to stay motivated and discover real world strategies to double your sales in a short amount of time. Hear from seasoned business entrepreneurs as well as her clients as they share what they did to make it happen. https://itunes.apple.com/us/podcast/double-your-sales-now-performance-selling-closing-sales/id1213169440?mt=2

ABOUT THE AUTHOR

Two-time Bestselling Author, Award winning Entrepreneur and Sales Expert—Ursula Mentjes—will transform the way you think about selling so you can reach your goals with less anxiety and less effort! The Founder of *Sales Coach Now* as well as an inspirational speaker, author of *Selling With Intention, Selling With Synchronicity* and *One Great Goal*— Ursula specializes in Neuro-Linguistic Programming to help clients double and triple their sales FAST.

Honing her skills at an international technical training company, where she began her career in 1996, Ursula increased sales by 90% in just one year! In 2001, when the company's annual run was in the tens of millions, Ursula advanced to the position of President at just 27 years old. Sales guru Brian Tracy endorsed *Selling With Intention*, saying, *"This powerful, practical book shows you how to connect with customers by fully understanding the sales process from the inside out. It really works!"* *Selling With Synchronicity* and *One Great Goal* were also the 2013 winners of the Beverly Hills Book Awards in the categories of sales and business motivation—and *Selling With Intention* was a finalist. *Selling With Intention* also received the International Book Award sponsored by USA Book News and *Selling With Synchronicity* was a finalist.

Ursula has also served as the Statewide Chairperson of the NAWBO-CA Education Fund and Past President of NAWBO-CA. She is the recipient of the SBA's 2014 Women in Business Champion, 2013 Willow Tree Extraordinary Example and Extraordinary Entrepreneur Awards, NAWBO-IE ANITA Award, chosen as PDP's Extraordinary Speaker of 2015, PDP's Business Woman of the Year 2016, the 2007 and 2011 Spirit of the Entrepreneur Awards Finalist, and recently received the President's Lifetime Achievement Award. She has shared the stage with Loral Langemeier, Les Brown, Tom Antion, Lisa Nichols, Giuliana Rancic, and many others. Her clients include Aflac, Ebenezer and Fairview Hospitals, New York Life, Paychex, and more. She holds a B.A. in Psychology and Communication from St. Olaf College and a M.S. in Counseling Psychology from California Baptist University.

CPSIA information can be obtained
at www.ICGtesting.com
Printed in the USA
FFOW02n1602170218
45058840-45446FF